BIRDING
CAPE COD

Illustrated by Barry Van Dusen
Maps by Janet Heywood

CAPE COD BIRD CLUB &

MASSACHUSETTS AUDUBON SOCIETY

Cover illustration copyright 1990 by John Sill.
Maps copyright 1990 by Janet Heywood.
Illustrations copyright 1990 by Barry Van Dusen.

Contributors: Janet Aylward, Sally Clifton, Richard Comeau, Blair Nikula, Robert Pease, Robert Prescott, Robert Scott, Charlotte Smith, Peter Trimble.

Edited by Gretchen Flock and Ann Prince Hecker.

Typesetting by Stevens Graphics, Brattleboro, Vermont.

Text and cover design by Martha E. Raines, Brattleboro, Vermont.

Produced by J. N. Townsend Publishing.

Published by Arey's Pond Press in association with the Massachusetts Audubon Society, Wellfleet Bay Wildlife Sanctuary, South Wellfleet, Massachusetts 02663.

Library of Congress Cataloging-in-Publication Data

Birding Cape Cod : guide to finding birds on Cape Cod / Massachusetts Audubon
   Society.
     p.   cm.
    Includes index.
    ISBN 0-9619485-1-5
    1. Bird watching—Massachusetts—Cape Cod—Guide-books.
I. Massachusetts Audubon Society.
QL684.M4B55   1989
598'.0723474492—dc20   89-6883
                                                CIP

ACKNOWLEDGMENTS

No project of this magnitude, written by a committee, could have been brought to fruition without the generous assistance of many people. It would be impossible to list all those who have contributed in ways both great and small, but we would like to thank those whose work was most important to the final product. First, and foremost, is Blair Nikula, without whose pushing, prodding, and rewriting, this book would still be unhatched in the nest of our imaginations. Bob Prescott, director of the Wellfleet Bay Wildlife Sanctuary, attended to the nearly endless and tedious details of production, and patiently bore the brunt of the contributors' frequent frustrations.

We also wish to thank Jim Baird and Richard Forster, who encouraged the project in its formative stages. Wayne Petersen contributed his many years of birding knowledge and expertise in reviewing the manuscript for accuracy and content. Jonnie Fisk, Diane Reynolds, Mike O'Connor, and John Redfern each offered assistance and insight at various stages of the project.

Finally, we appreciate the patience and advice of Jeremy Townsend as she led us through the unfamiliar maze of publishing decisions on the way to the successful fledging of this book.

DEDICATION

This book is dedicated to Charlotte Smith, heart and soul of the Cape Cod Bird Club. With good humor and patience, she has introduced an uncounted number of people to the joy of birding on Cape Cod.

ALSO . . .

In memory of Jonnie Fisk, one of this book's benefactors, who passed away before it fledged. Known to biologists and naturalists for her work as a bird bander and tern warden, Jonnie led a full and interesting life. She inspired many, encouraging even more, and entertained legions with her books, lectures and banding demonstrations. All of her friends and fans will certainly miss her.

TABLE OF CONTENTS

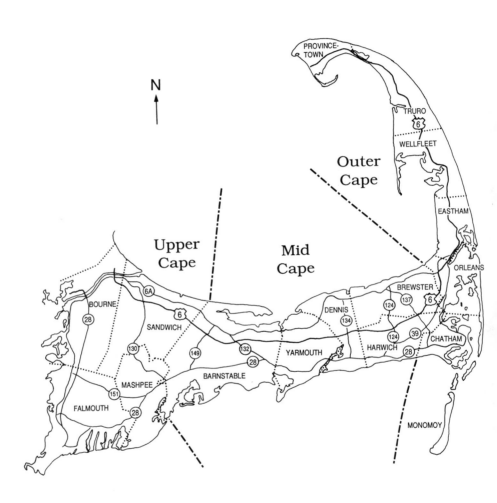

N

Outer
Cape

Upper
Cape

Mid
Cape

PROVINCE-
TOWN

TRURO
6

WELLFLEET

EASTHAM

ORLEANS

BREWSTER
124 137 6

DENNIS
134

124 39 CHATHAM

HARWICH
28

BARNSTABLE

YARMOUTH

6A

BOURNE
28

SANDWICH
6

130

149

132

28

MASHPEE
151

FALMOUTH
28

MONOMOY

INTRODUCTION

The "bare and bended arm" of Cape Cod extends eastward for 25 miles from the mainland of Massachusetts, thence northward for another 30 miles to its terminus in Provincetown, and is at no point more than 10 miles wide. The sights and sounds of the sea are never far away. The peninsula is composed of glacial outwash from the final stages of the Pleistocene epoch 10,000 years ago, making it very young in a geological sense.

Despite its relative youth, the Cape, as it is known locally and referred to throughout this book, has the oldest recorded ornithological history in North America. As early as 1602 the explorer Bartholomew Gosnold, who is credited with discovering Cape Cod, wrote of a bird in local waters that came to be known as the Great Auk. Three years later Samuel de Champlain described what were almost certainly Black Skimmers in the Nauset area. During the 1800s the peninsula's birdlife was studied and observed by such noted naturalists as William Brewster, Edward Howe Forbush, Arthur Cleveland Bent, C. B. Cory, and Henry Thoreau.

During the first half of this century, the renowned Ludlow Griscom owned a home in Chatham and spent a great deal of time birding on the Cape with various other luminaries of his time. Also during that period, the Austin Ornithological Station was established at what is now the Wellfleet Bay Wildlife Sanctuary. The Cape's popularity among both amateur and professional ornithologists continued unabated, and in 1965 two publications chronicling the area's bird life appeared: "The Birds of Cape Cod," by Norman Hill and "The Birds of the Cape Cod National Seashore," by Wallace Bailey.

Despite this high level of interest and the proliferation of bird-finding guides nationwide, no guide appeared for birdfinding here. This effort fills that gap.

WHEN TO COME

Cape Cod offers the possibility of good birding in any season, though fall has traditionally been the most popular among visiting birders. There is no wrong time to visit because in any season there is a diverse array of species and always the chance for something unusual.

Spring brings a rush of northbound shorebirds, sea ducks, hawks and songbirds. Historically, spring was considered to be the poorest of seasons in this area, with little to see other than a nice shorebird migration. In the *Birds of Cape Cod,* Hill described the spring migration of land birds as "predictably unimpressive." Two and a half decades later it is clear that his characterization was overly disparaging. Increased birding activity in the spring has shown that the Cape hosts an excellent array of northbound pas-serines, as well as hawks, and at times the number of birds can be very impressive. Though it is true that the magnitude of the migra-tion over the peninsula is far less than over the mainland (as shown by radar studies conducted in North Truro in the late 1960s), the topography of the peninsula, narrowing progressively eastward, then northward, as it does, results in a concentration of northbound birds as they move "out" the Cape and eventually encounter an expanse of water blocking their flight path. Birders can thus be treated to some fine displays of migrants, particularly from Wellfleet northward, with the largest concentrations typically culminating in Provincetown. Peak numbers of most species occur, on average, several days behind peaks on the mainland, but the foliage lags even further behind, so that most of the birds pass through before the trees are fully leaved, making them easier to see than at most inland sites.

Summer, if you can bear the overwhelming human tide, offers a number of interesting nesting species, as well as various non-breeding visitors and the bulk of the southward shorebird migration. Approximately 130 species nest locally and, although the diversity of upland breeding birds is less, some species are more common and easier to find on the Cape than on the mainland. Several note-worthy coastal species, including Piping Plover, Roseate and Arctic Terns, and occasionally Black Skimmer, nest on some of the barrier beaches and islands. Pelagic birds, particularly those species, such as Wilson's Storm-Petrel and Sooty and Greater Shearwaters, that nest in the south Atlantic, are common offshore. Other nonbreeding visitors in this season include some of the southern herons (e.g., Tricolored and Little Blue Herons, Great Egret, and Yellow-crowned Night-Heron) and southern terns (e.g., Royal and Sandwich Terns). The first of the southbound shorebirds often appear by the end of June, and their migration is in full swing by mid-July. The fall migration of warblers and various other songbirds begins as early as late July with the first waterthrushes and Yellow Warblers and builds during August.

In fall a steady stream of songbirds passes through, the numbers varying considerably depending on the weather condi-tions. The bulk of the thrushes, vireos, and warblers appear in

September, followed by kinglets, sparrows, blackbirds, and others in October. The first Peregrines, Merlins, and accipiters arrive by mid-September and are seen regularly into November. This is also the time to look for some of the rare but regular western vagrants, including Western Kingbird, Dickcissel, Clay-colored and Lark Sparrows, and Yellow-headed Blackbird. Although the number of shorebirds present begins to drop dramatically early in the fall, the variety reaches its peak in September as a few of the rarer species, such as Lesser Golden-Plover, and Buff-breasted and Baird's Sand-pipers, appear. Offshore, the pelagic diversity also peaks as the arctic-nesting species, such as jaegers and phalaropes, join the dwindling ranks of shearwaters and storm-petrels. In October large flights of sea ducks appear, predominately scoters initially, followed by eiders and oldsquaws in November. Large numbers of gannets also slice down the coast during the late fall, providing one of the area's exciting avian spectacles. Birding in this season is always enhanced by the knowledge that almost anything can show up—a fact proven time and again!

Many of the Cape's residents believe that winter is the best of seasons, as the beaches are largely vacant, and for a short while a sense of peace prevails. The birder can find much of interest as well, because a variety of northern species combine with lingering "half-hardies" to produce a diverse avian potpourri. Wintering ducks settle into their preferred haunts, both along the coast and on freshwater ponds. Alcids, predominantly Razorbills, may appear in quantity along with a few Iceland and Glaucous Gulls. Northern "irruptive" species, such as Rough-legged Hawk, Snowy Owl, Northern Shrike, and the boreal finches, may appear, though their numbers vary unpredictably from year to year. The peninsula's slightly warmer climate and abundance of fruit-bearing shrubs induce a variety of species to linger later than they do on the mainland. By carefully birding the appropriate thickets it is possible to find catbirds, towhees, robins, Hermit Thrushes, Yellow-breasted Chats, and others.

HABITATS

The Cape's habitats have all been heavily affected both by humans and the marine environment. Early accounts indicate that most of the peninsula was heavily forested at the time of the Euro-peans arrival in the area in the 1600s. However, by the late 1800s the Cape had been largely clear-cut, and few trees remained. During the first half of this century, as agriculture diminished and fires were increasingly suppressed, the woodlands regenerated; today, most of the undeveloped land remaining is wooded with second growth forest.

In natural upland habitat succession in this area, open fields and pastures gradually grow up in shrubs, red cedar, and cherry. In time, pitch pine takes hold and eventually shades out the smaller trees and shrubs. As the pitch pine barrens mature, and when fires are absent, oaks begin to invade and, as they mature, shade out the pines. In the final stage, rarely achieved on the Cape in recent times, the oak forest gives way to one in which beech becomes the climax species. Unfortunately, the climax habitat on Cape Cod today is all too often characterized by extensive tracts of asphalt and shopping malls.

Most of the area's woodlands today are in a transitional state between pine and oak, and this is by far the most widespread upland habitat. The openness that characterized the Cape at the turn of the century has largely vanished. Fields and pastures are all but gone, having been either bulldozed under or, lacking fires or periodic mowing to keep them open, succeeded to subsequent vegetational stages. Pitch pine barrens too are very fire-dependent and are fast disappearing. In a few, small, isolated patches, primarily in the upper Cape, near-climax beech woodlands exist.

Among the Cape's freshwater habitats are over 300 ponds which range in size from less than an acre to over 700 acres, several small rivers, and a number of small white cedar and/or red maple swamps.

The area's marine environments are characterized by numerous bays, harbors, and estuaries. All of these embayments are bordered, at least in part, by parcels of salt marsh, in some cases comprising only an acre or two, in others, vast expanses encompassing many hundreds of acres, such as the Great Marsh in Barnstable. Most of these areas are separated from the open water by barrier spits or islands, also of greatly varying size. The smaller spits are typically sparsely vegetated with beach grass and a few other marine-adapted plants and shrubs, while the larger spits, such as Sandy Neck in Barnstable, may contain small patches of woodland in their sheltered dune hollows.

The following are characteristic *breeding* bird species of the major habitats.

Residential areas:

Rock Dove
Mourning Dove
Chimney Swift
Eastern Phoebe (uncommon)
Barn Swallow
Carolina Wren (uncommon)
House Wren (uncommon)
American Robin
Gray Catbird
House Sparrow

European Starling
Northern Cardinal
Chipping Sparrow
Song Sparrow
Common Grackle
Brown-headed Cowbird
Orchard Oriole (rare)
Northern Oriole
House Finch

Fields, pastures, moors, and edges:

Green-backed Heron
(uncommon)
American Kestrel
Ring-necked Pheasant
Northern Bobwhite
American Woodcock
Black-billed Cuckoo
(uncommon)
Willow Flycatcher (rare)
Eastern Kingbird
Tree Swallow
Eastern Bluebird (rare)
Northern Mockingbird
Cedar Waxwing

Brown Thrasher
(uncommon)
Yellow Warbler
Prairie Warbler
Common Yellowthroat
Indigo Bunting (rare)
Field Sparrow
Vesper Sparrow (rare)
Savannah Sparrow
Grasshopper Sparrow
(rare)
Red-winged Blackbird
Eastern Meadowlark
American Goldfinch

All woodlands:

Red-tailed Hawk
Great Horned Owl
Downy Woodpecker
Northern Flicker

Blue Jay
Common Crow
Black-capped Chickadee
Rufous-sided Towhee

Pitch pine barrens:

Northern Saw-whet Owl (rare)
Whip-poor-will
Red-breasted Nuthatch
(uncommon)
Hermit Thrush (uncommon)

Pine Warbler
Prairie Warbler
Chipping Sparrow
Purple Finch

Mixed pine/oak woodlands:

Broad-winged Hawk
Ruffed Grouse
Yellow-billed Cuckoo
(uncommon)
Eastern Screech-Owl
Whip-poor-will
Hairy Woodpecker
Eastern Wood-Pewee
Great Crested Flycatcher
Tufted Titmouse

Red-breasted Nuthatch
White-breasted Nuthatch
Brown Creeper
(uncommon)
Wood Thrush
Red-eyed Vireo
Black-and-White Warbler
Ovenbird
Scarlet Tanager
Northern Oriole

Freshwater marshes:

Mute Swan
Canada Goose
American Black Duck
Mallard
Virginia Rail (rare)
Belted Kingfisher

Marsh Wren
Swamp Sparrow
Red-winged Blackbird
Yellow Warbler
Common Yellowthroat

Salt marshes:

Osprey (uncommon)
American Oystercatcher
(uncommon)
Willet (uncommon)

Sharp-tailed Sparrow
Seaside Sparrow
Red-winged Blackbird

Dunes and beaches:

Northern Harrier (rare)
Piping Plover
Laughing Gull (uncommon)
Herring Gull
Great Black-backed Gull
Horned Lark

Roseate Tern
(uncommon)
Common Tern
Arctic Tern (rare)
Least Tern
Savannah Sparrow

CLIMATE

Cape Cod enjoys, or suffers, depending upon the season and your point of view, a maritime climate. Temperatures are ameliorated by the surrounding water with the result that summers are cooler and winters milder than the adjacent mainland—temperature extremes are not so extreme out here.

Winters typically feature raw, damp, and windy weather, though there are frequent exceptions to this pattern. The relatively warm water surrounding the peninsula keeps air temperatures a few degrees above those on the mainland and often results in the Cape receiving rain while it is snowing inland. Although snowfall on the Cape averages less than on the mainland, major snowstorms do indeed occur, and when coastal storms pass far enough to the east, it is quite possible for the Cape to be buried under a foot or more of snow while Boston receives only a couple of inches.

Spring is the cruelest of seasons locally, frequently offering little more than unfulfilled expectations. Indeed, local dogma is that the Cape has only three (and some would argue only two) seasons, and spring is not one of them! The ocean turns from ally to enemy in this season, as the waters are much slower than the land to relinquish the winter's chill, and the persistent onshore breezes keep temperatures as much as 15 to 20 degrees, and on rare occasions even 30 degrees, below those away from the water. Not only is the wind cooler, it is also moisture laden, and fog becomes prevalent as the sharp temperature differential between water and air causes condensation. All too often mainlanders bask in sunny warmth while Cape Codders shiver in a damp soup! Such weather extremes occur frequently even within the Cape as the north side, which is several miles "inland" from the prevailing southerly winds, can experience very pleasant conditions while a cool fog hangs along the south shore. Indeed, Chatham suffers the dubious distinction of being one of the fog capitals of the East Coast.

During summer, the cool sea breezes turn friendly again and keep the Cape from cooking. Heat waves that bake the mainland in 90 plus degree temperatures rarely push the mercury much above 80 degrees locally. Fog remains persistent early in the season but gradually wanes as the surrounding waters finally warm a bit and the temperature differential diminishes.

Falls are long and delightful. Water temperatures peak early in the season, and the air turns cool and dry. Migrant birds pass through in great diversity and abundance and produce some of the best birding of the year. The locals agree that this is *the* time of the year to be on the Cape. Unfortunately, the secret is out, and the summer congestion now lingers well into autumn.

GETTING AROUND

From the Cape Cod Canal, three main roads, Routes 6, 6A, and 28, run in a generally eastward direction to Orleans. Route 6 (also called the Mid-Cape Highway) is the major highway, limited-access and double-barrelled for much of its length, and runs down the terminal moraine—the "backbone" of the Cape. It is by far the fastest and most direct route to many destinations, natural and otherwise.

Route 6A is a scenic, two-lane road, lined with lovely old homes, that winds along the north side of the peninsula. Travel along Route 6A can be painfully slow during the tourist season, but it is a beautiful drive through most of its length and affords access to many fine birding spots on the Cape Cod Bay shore.

Route 28 runs south from the canal to Falmouth, then east along the south shore of the Cape to Chatham, and finally north to Orleans. Through much of its length, it is a heavily congested, two-lane road which penetrates some of the most developed commercial sections of the Cape. During the tourist season Route 28 can be almost impassable at times, particularly on rainy days when everyone seems to be skipping from one of the infinite number of gift shops to the next, and in the late afternoons and early evenings when people leave the beaches en masse and head out to dinner. At those times, portions of the road in Falmouth, Hyannis, and Yarmouth can be virtually gridlocked. During the off-season the road becomes more tolerable, and it does provide access to many fine birding locales along the Nantucket Sound shoreline.

Five main roads, Routes 130, 149, 134, and 137, all running on a generally north-south axis, connect Routes 6A, 6, and 28. From Orleans to Provincetown, Route 6 is the only highway. This stretch of the highway, particularly through the town of Eastham, is congested and very dangerous—drive it with extreme caution.

Although it is not difficult to get lost on the old, winding side roads, you can take comfort in the fact that it is not possible to travel far without hitting one of the main highways—or the water!

A variety of maps is available at any local newsstand, pharmacy, supermarket, etc., the most popular of which, among local birders, is the Miller's Cape Cod Atlas and Guide Book, put out by the Butterworth Company. It is updated annually: an important consideration in this rapidly developing area.

A source of much confusion is the local usage of the terms "outer Cape," "lower Cape," "mid-Cape," "upper Cape," and "inner Cape" to describe various regions of the peninsula. Ask any five residents to explain these colloquialisms, and you'll likely get at least five different answers. The terms are widely used but have no clear, universally accepted definitions. "Outer" and "lower" are synonymous and refer to the outermost (i.e., farthest from the main-land) portion of the Cape, generally Chatham to Provincetown, but occasionally including Brewster and Harwich. The rationale, if any, behind the description lower to describe this section of the Cape is unknown, but certainly has no connection with its location on a map. The "mid-Cape" usually refers to the area from Dennis to Barnstable. The "upper" or, less commonly, "inner" Cape encom-passes Sandwich, Bourne, Falmouth, Mashpee, and, in some cases, Barnstable.

BEACH ACCESS

Most of the beaches described in this book are either town, state, or federally owned and are open to the public. During the peak tourist season, from mid-June through Labor Day, virtually all charge an admission/parking fee. In many cases, it is possible to purchase weekly or seasonal passes which, if you are planning an extended stay, can be a worthwhile investment.

However, most beach tollbooths are operated from about 9 AM to 5 PM, and only on good beach days. Consequently, you can usually avoid both the fees and the disruptive hordes of sun-worshiping humanity by planning to visit these areas early in the morning or early in the evening, when the birds are both less dis-turbed and more active. Rainy days also offer a less costly and often more productive birding alternative.

THE TIDES AND THE "OCEAN"

The tides are a critical component in the lives of many Cape Codders, and birders are no exception. The tides in this area, as elsewhere on the East Coast, are semidiurnal: two cycles per day, each about 12.5 hours in duration, making a total of two high and two low tides every 25 hours (approximately).

Most of the local newspapers publish daily or weekly tide charts, and any marina or sporting goods store can supply an annual chart. Many of the charts use Boston tides as a reference and provide a conversion factor for various local sites. In general, tides along the shores of Cape Cod Bay are about 10 to 15 minutes later than Boston; along the oceanside beaches from Provincetown to Chatham they are about 30 minutes later, and along Nantucket Sound, about 45 minutes to an hour or so later. Additionally, in the larger estuaries, such as Pleasant Bay, Nauset Marsh, and the Sandy Neck marsh, the tide in the upper portions of the estuary can lag as much as a couple of hours behind the mouth of the estuary. Average tidal ranges on the Cape vary from nearly ten feet in Wellfleet to two feet or less in the Falmouth area.

The tides are a concern to birders primarily when they are looking for shorebirds. The best tides depend on the location and whether the birds use the area primarily for feeding or roosting. When the tide is a factor at a site, we have indicated so in the text.

The term "ocean" is bandied about a great deal in casual conversation on Cape Cod. Cape Cod Bay is a large and rather impressive body of saltwater, as is Nantucket Sound; however, neither is *the* ocean. Anyone who has spent much time in a boat on the true ocean knows the difference very well. To see the real ocean, you must be on the eastern shore of the Cape from Provincetown south to Chatham—nowhere else!

PESTS

Although there are no poisonous snakes or reptiles, nor any dangerous carnivores, Cape Cod does have its share of biting insects, and, during the warmer months, you will do well to arm yourself with an appropriate repellent.

Ticks are perhaps the most serious concern. Two species are present on the Cape: the larger, more frequently encountered, and relatively innocuous dog tick (*Dermacentor variabilis*), and the tiny, dangerous, and nearly undetectable deer tick (*Ixodes dammini*).

The deer tick is a carrier of Lyme disease which, if untreated, can result in severe arthritis-like conditions as well as cardiac and neurological symptoms. Deer ticks are the size of a pinhead and very difficult to spot. Prior to walking through grassy areas, tuck your pant legs into your socks, and spray your ankles with repellent. Perhaps your best defense is to be aware of the disease's early symptoms: a red ring or rash around the bite and/or flulike symptoms. If detected and attended to early enough, Lyme disease usually can be treated effectively with antibiotics, usually with no long-term effects.

Mosquitoes are common and widespread throughout the warmer months (May to September), though rarely reaching the intolerable levels that well-traveled birders have probably experienced elsewhere. Greenhead flies (*Tabanus sp.*) can be a serious nuisance around the region's salt marshes in mid-summer. Fortunately, they have a short season, usually from mid-July through mid-August, and the bite, though painful and often bloody, disappears quickly, usually without aftereffects. The wooden boxes placed around the upper edges of many local salt marshes during the summer, typically blue or green in color and about four cubic feet in dimension, are traps designed to reduce the number of these man-eaters. Deer flies, cousins of the greenhead, patrol upland areas and are equally voracious and persistent, though equally harmless in the long run.

At dawn and dusk on still, warm summer days, nearly invisible clouds of minuscule "no-see-ums," or biting midges (*Ceratopogonidae sp.*) emerge to bedevil anyone out and about during those periods. They, too, concentrate around salt marshes and have a bite that is all out of proportion to their size but, again, a bite that is short-lived. To make matters worse, these tiny terrors seem totally oblivious to most commercial repellents and are extremely skilled at finding the smallest patch of exposed skin.

LOCAL ORGANIZATIONS

The Cape Cod Bird Club conducts several walks each month and holds meetings on the second Monday night of each month, from September through May, at the Cape Cod Museum of Natural History in Brewster. Visitors are always welcome at all club activities; check the local papers for current listings.

Massachusetts Audubon's Wellfleet Bay Wildlife Sanctuary in South Wellfleet (508-349-2615) and the Cape Cod Museum of Natural History in Brewster (508-896-3867) both conduct guided bird walks on a regular basis, usually for a nominal fee. Contact them for their current schedules, or check the listings in the local papers.

The Bird Watcher's General Store in Orleans (508-255-6974) serves as a local clearinghouse for bird sightings, particularly those from the outer Cape. Massachusetts Audubon's "Voice of Audubon" (617-259-8805) is a tape-recorded message of recent bird sightings throughout Massachusetts and often includes reports from Cape Cod.

Anyone finding an unusual bird in the area should contact the Wellfleet Bay Wildlife Sanctuary, the Bird Watcher's General Store, or the Cape Cod Museum of Natural History.

USING THIS BOOK

In the site descriptions that follow, we have attempted to reduce the amount of tedious, written road directions by relying heavily upon high quality maps. In our experience, a clearly drawn map is worth many hundreds of words. Written directions are limited to those situations in which a map cannot adequately convey the information necessary to guide the visitor. If you find an area in which you feel this system has fallen short, please let us know.

Any publication of this sort, particularly one covering as rapidly a developing area as Cape Cod, is doomed to an early obsolescence. We have attempted to postpone this inevitability to the greatest degree possible by limiting coverage primarily to sites that are publicly owned and thus, we trust, protected into the foreseeable future. Privately owned sites have generally been excluded, except in the few instances where there is reason to believe they will remain in a natural state well into the future, and where the owners have been particularly tolerant of visitors.

Nevertheless, changes in the local avifauna and habitats are as inevitable as time and tides. If you detect any changes, or errors in any aspect of this publication, or have any suggestions to offer, we encourage you to write to the Cape Cod Bird Club, c/o Cape Cod Museum of Natural History, P. O. Drawer R, Brewster, MA 02631. Good birding!

BIRDING
CAPE COD

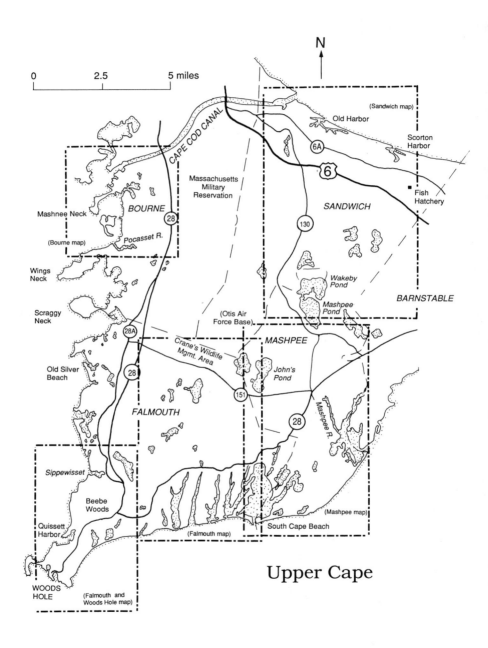

N

0   2.5   5 miles

CAPE COD CANAL

(Sandwich map)

Old Harbor

Scorton
Harbor

6A

6

Massachusetts
Military
Reservation

Fish
Hatchery

SANDWICH

Mashnee Neck

BOURNE

28

(Bourne map)

Pocasset R.

130

Wings
Neck

Wakeby
Pond

BARNSTABLE

Scraggy
Neck

Mashpee
Pond

28A

(Otis Air
Force Base)

MASHPEE

Old Silver
Beach

28

Crane's Wildlife
Mgmt. Area

John's
Pond

151

FALMOUTH

28

Mashpee R.

Sippewisset

Beebe
Woods

(Mashpee map)

Quissett
Harbor

South Cape Beach

(Falmouth map)

WOODS
HOLE

(Falmouth and
Woods Hole map)

Upper Cape

1 THE UPPER CAPE

The area we have defined as the Upper Cape encompasses the towns of Bourne, Sandwich, Falmouth, and Mashpee. Primary attractions for the birder are the extensive shorelines on Cape Cod Bay, Buzzards Bay, and Nantucket Sound, which provide ample opportunities to see wintering seabirds; the numerous fresh- and saltwater ponds, particularly in the Falmouth area, which attract large numbers of wintering ducks; and a variety of upland habitats, some of which host a few of the Cape's more unusual breeding passerine species.

BOURNE

Bourne straddles the west end of the Cape Cod Canal. Primary birding areas in the town are the necks that extend into Buzzards Bay, the Bourne Town Forest, and the Pocasset River system.

Mashnee Neck (Hog Island) is a peninsula extending into Buzzards Bay that can provide excellent views of loons, grebes cormorants, sea ducks, gulls, and terns. During the winter Common Eiders raft in large numbers north of the neck along with Common Goldeneyes and rarely a King Eider or Barrow's Goldeneye. South of the neck, Horned Grebes, Buffleheads, scaup, scoters, and other sea ducks can be seen.

The **Bourne Town Forest** is comprised of white pine, pitch pine and oaks. Black-billed and Yellow-billed Cuckoos, Wood Thrushes, Brown Thrashers, Pine and Prairie Warblers, Scarlet Tanagers, and rarely an Eastern Bluebird or an Eastern Screech-Owl can be found while hiking through the woods during the nesting season. Park on Valley Bar Road; dirt roads cross the forest, allowing easy access throughout.

The **Pocasset River (Four Ponds Conservation Area)** has a series of trails that offer fine birding all year. The ponds are connected by the Pocasset River and often have Buffleheads and Ring-necked Ducks in season. During the breeding season, Pine Warblers may be found, and Prairie Warblers should be listened for in the drier pine woods. White-breasted and Red-breasted Nuthatches, Brown Creepers, and Golden-crowned Kinglets are likely to be present during the winter. Access is available from Barlow's Landing Road; watch for the small parking area by a sign marking the Four Ponds Conservation Area.

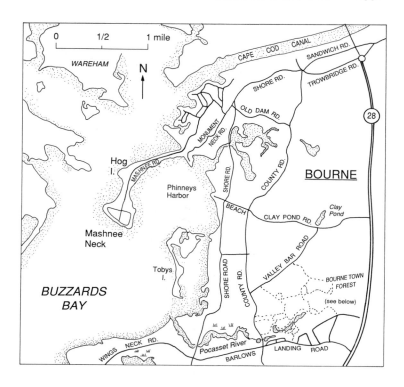

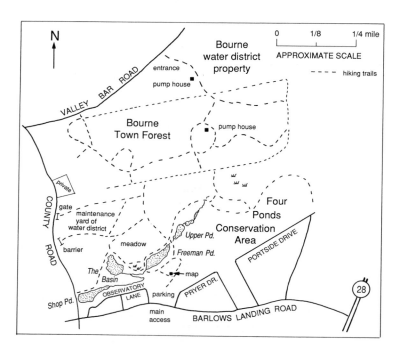

FALMOUTH & WOODS HOLE

Falmouth is a great spot to bird throughout the year. Of particular interest are the many ponds that harbor a great variety of wintering waterfowl. Lingering fall migrants and semi-hardy land birds attempt to overwinter in the numerous thickets. Additionally, there are coastal lookouts, estuaries, fields, woods, and a bike path that connects several birding areas from Woods Hole through Nobska Point to Oyster and Salt Ponds.

Little Sippewisset (Wood Neck Road marsh) is a small marsh providing a niche for herons, egrets, Belted Kingfishers, Sharp-tailed Sparrows, and (occasionally) rails. At the end of Wood Neck Road is a view of Buzzards Bay where cormorants, gulls, terns, and wintering sea ducks can be found.

Quissett Harbor (The Knob) has wintering waterfowl, which are often at close range for viewing. Horned Grebes, Common Eiders, Oldsquaws, White-winged, Surf, and Black Scoters, Common Goldeneyes, and Red-breasted Mergansers feed in the waters off the Knob. From the end of the Knob check for Roseate and Least Terns during the summer. Land birds such as Carolina Wrens, Hermit Thrushes and Gray Catbirds can sometimes be seen in season. Parking is available near the end of Quissett Harbor Road. From there, look for the sign indicating "Salt Pond Bird Sanctuary" and follow the trail out the peninsula.

MBL Beach affords a great view of Buzzards Bay; scoters, eiders, mergansers, and Oldsquaws are often present in numbers.

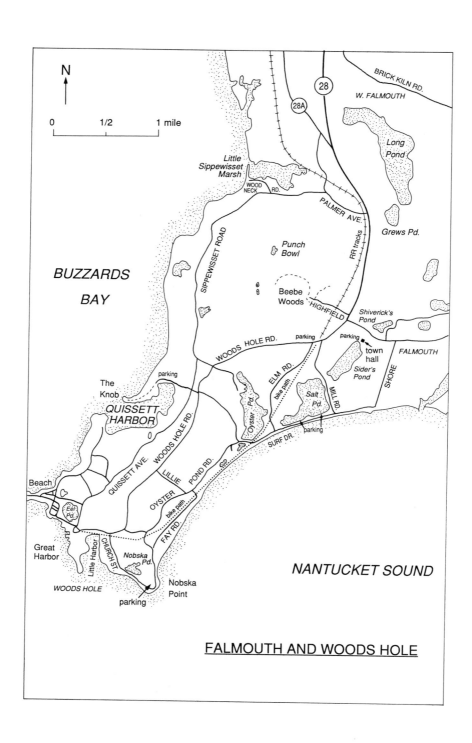

N

0   1/2   1 mile

BRICK KILN RD.

W. FALMOUTH

28

28A

Long Pond

Little Sippewisset Marsh

WOOD NECK RD.

PALMER AVE.

Grews Pd.

SIPPEWISSET ROAD

Punch Bowl

RR tracks

BUZZARDS BAY

Beebe Woods

HIGHFIELD

Shiverick's Pond

WOODS HOLE RD.

parking

parking

town hall

FALMOUTH

Sider's Pond

ELM RD.

The Knob

parking

bike path

Salt Pd.

MILL RD.

SHORE

QUISSETT HARBOR

Oyster Pd.

WOODS HOLE RD.

parking

SURF DR.

QUISSETT AVE.

LILLIE

POND RD.

Beach

OYSTER

bike path

Eel Pd.

FAY RD.

Great Harbor

CHURCH ST.

Little Harbor

Nobska Pd.

NANTUCKET SOUND

WOODS HOLE

Nobska Point

parking

FALMOUTH AND WOODS HOLE

Woods Hole Harbor (Great Harbor) is famous for being home to the Woods Hole Oceanographic Institution, the Marine Biological Laboratory, and the National Marine Fisheries. Woods Hole is an interesting town with some fine restaurants, but is a very congested area with limited parking. During the off season, however, it is usually possible to find a parking spot in town and then walk out to the harbor.

Great and Double-crested Cormorants, sea ducks, Purple Sandpipers, gulls, and Harbor Seals are some of the natural attractions. Iceland Gulls are regular winter visitors and Glaucous, Black-headed, and Little Gulls have been found on rare occasions. Great Cormorants in winter and Double-crested Cormorants in summer fish the harbor and dry off on the exposed rocks. Common Eiders are the most numerous of the wintering ducks, although a few scoters and rarely a Barrow's Goldeneye or King Eider are present as well.

The **Nobska Point** area consists of three sections: Nobska Pond, the lookout at the Coast Guard station, and the Woods Hole to Oyster Pond bike path. Nobska Pond is surrounded by thickets that often harbor migrant and wintering land birds. Mute Swans are usually present on the pond and sometimes a few Hooded Mergansers, but rarely is there anything else. The lookout at the point offers a wide view of Nantucket Sound, with the Elizabeth Islands to the west, and Martha's Vineyard to the south. Cormorants, Common and Red-throated Loons, Horned Grebes, Common Eiders, scoters, Red-breasted Mergansers, and gulls may be observed from this prominent bluff, and Purple Sandpipers have been spotted on the rocks below. On rare occasions during the colder months, Little and Black-headed Gulls have been seen among the more common Bonaparte's Gulls, and in the deeper water to the southeast alcids are a remote possibility. The bike path affords good birding along its entire length. (Take care where you park.) Check for land birds in the early morning during migration and in early winter. As in most of Falmouth, the thickets along this route and the roads that cross it often contain semi-hardy wintering birds, such as Carolina Wrens, Hermit Thrushes, catbirds, and towhees.

Oyster Pond and **Salt Pond** are accessible from the bike path that passes south of Oyster Pond and along the north side of Salt Pond. To cover the entire path on foot requires considerable time.

The habitat bordering Nantucket Sound consists of thickets, marshes, ponds, small open areas and deciduous woodlands. Year-round, this region is a worthwhile birding spot and is an enjoyable place to walk or ride. In particular, search the thickets around the

ponds and marshes, which often host Carolina Wrens, Cedar Waxwings, sparrows, and other land birds. In early winter, a Yellow-
breasted Chat, Orange-crowned Warbler or some other unusual
species will appear on occasion. White-eyed Vireos have nested in
this area and woodcocks perform their mating flights along the bike
path. Although both ponds are good places to find wintering waterfowl, Salt Pond generally has more birds and can be checked from
Mill Road, Surf Drive, or the bike path. Species frequently present
include Great and Double-crested Cormorants, Canvasback,
Greater Scaup, Common Goldeneye, Bufflehead, and Hooded
Merganser. Redheads, though less common, are found regularly.
The flocks of Ring-billed Gulls should be scanned carefully for Little
and Black-headed Gulls, as both have been sighted here.

  Beebe Woods is a large stretch of deciduous woods in which
forest species such as Wood Thrush, Ovenbird, and Scarlet Tanager
nest. House Wrens nest around the summer theater buildings and
may be heard and watched as they move about the grounds. The
thickets and trees around the buildings and at the beginning of the
woods trail should be checked for a variety of passerines. The
lengthy trail is usually not very productive, but offers a rigorous walk
through lovely woods. Park in the conservatory parking lot at the end
of Highfield Drive.

  Sider's Pond and **Shiverick's Pond** are excellent sites for ducks
in the late fall, winter, and early spring. Species found here include
Pied-billed Grebe, Great and Double-crested Cormorants, Red-
head, Canvasback, Greater and Lesser Scaup, Ring-necked Duck,
Common Goldeneye, Hooded Merganser, and American Coot.
Also, Sider's Pond has fine thickets located behind the Falmouth
Town Hall that are a stopping place for land birds during fall, winter,
and spring. Check Sider's Pond from the parking lot behind the town
hall and Shiverick's from Katherine Lee Bates Road in the center
of town.

  Little Pond, Great Pond, Green Pond, and **Bournes Pond** are
among the more productive of the town's brackish coastal ponds
and in winter should be searched carefully for Canvasbacks, Redheads, scaup, and Hooded and Common Mergansers. The edges of
these ponds and the rivers and streams that feed into them are good
birding spots where accessible. For example, the northern end of
Great Pond where the Coonamessett River enters at Route 28
should be checked for sparrows and other birds during the fall and
winter.

Mill Pond in East Falmouth usually has an interesting mix of wintering ducks, often including wigeon. Check it from behind the East Falmouth Library off Route 28.

The **Child's River**, where it crosses Cross Road, is another good spot to check in the winter for ducks, particularly Green-winged Teal and Hooded Mergansers, kingfishers and a heron or two.

Dutchman's Ditch is a small conservation area that contains woodlands, marsh, ponds, and cranberry bogs. The ponds can be good for Pied-billed Grebes, Mute Swans, Green-winged Teal, Gadwalls, American Wigeon, Ring-necked Ducks, and American Coots. The woods may have migrant passerines and during winter can have Hermit Thrushes, Brown Creepers, Golden-crowned Kinglets and Pine Warblers. The first swallows, blackbirds, and other migrants of the spring often are found here. Access is from John Parker Road, a few hundred yards south of Sandwich Road; watch for a couple of narrow, rutted dirt roads that lead a short way into the ponds.

The **Ashumet Holly Reservation**, a Massachusetts Audubon Society wildlife sanctuary, is a beautiful spot where several varieties of hollies, club mosses, and various aquatic plants are but a portion of a special botanical landscape and contribute to a pleasant birding experience. The fields may hold migrant Bobolinks, Indigo Buntings, and sparrows in season and the many thickets and woodlands harbor most of the common land birds including Carolina Wrens and Pine Warblers. The abundant fruit crop usually attracts flocks of wintering Robins and Cedar Waxwings as well as a few "halfhardies" such as Gray Catbirds and Hermit Thrushes. In summer there is a Barn Swallow colony in the maintenance building and Orchard Orioles appear in some years.

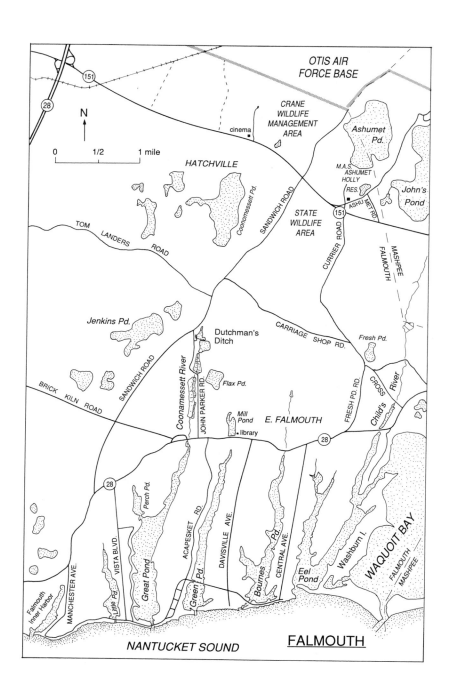

The **Crane Wildlife Management Area,** a large tract managed for Northern Bobwhites and Ring-necked Pheasants, by the Massachusetts Division of Fisheries and Wildlife, has extensive pine barrens and fields, broken by numerous planted hedgerows. This is one of the last places on Cape Cod where nesting Grasshopper Sparrows and Eastern Meadowlarks can be found. Eastern Bluebirds are sometimes seen here as well. Prairie Warblers and Field Sparrows are common nesting birds along the field edges, and during migration Northern Harriers, Upland Sandpipers, Vesper Sparrows and Bobolinks might be found in the fields. In the wooded portions of the area, Broad-winged and Red-tailed Hawks, Ruffed Grouse, Great Horned Owls, Yellow-billed Cuckoos, Hermit Thrushes, Pine Warblers, and Scarlet Tanagers nest. Look for Black-billed Cuckoos, Brown Thrashers, and Indigo Buntings in the woodland clearings.

A couple of parking areas are available on the north side of Route 151, one just to the east of the Nickelodeon Cinema, the other just to the west; watch for the brown Massachusetts Division of Fisheries and Wildlife's Wildlife Management Area signs.

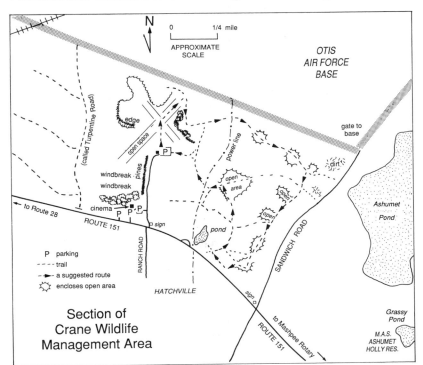

N

0   1/4 mile

APPROXIMATE
SCALE

OTIS
AIR FORCE
BASE

(called Turpentine Road)

edge

open space

gate to base

power line

windbreak — pines

windbreak

open area

dirt

to Route 28

cinema   P P P

ROUTE 151

sign

pond

open

open

Ashumet
Pond

RANCH ROAD

SANDWICH ROAD

P   parking
- - - trail
- ►- a suggested route
encloses open area

HATCHVILLE

sign

to Mashpee Rotary

ROUTE 151

Grassy
Pond

M.A.S.
ASHUMET
HOLLY RES.

Section of Crane Wildlife Management Area

SANDWICH

The town of Sandwich, one of the fastest growing on the Cape, has extensive salt marshes, a few freshwater ponds, tracts of deciduous woods, bogs, dense stands of red cedar, impenetrable thickets, widely varied vegetation, and a ridge that rises to 200 feet above sea level. You will also find exceptional views of Cape Cod Bay.

The **Sandwich Marina** and the east end of the canal around the jetty are good places to watch gulls during the winter, and thousands of eiders gather just south of the jetty. During and after fall storms, storm-petrels and shearwaters often can be seen out over the bay.

The **Boardwalk** in Sandwich is a good place to see shorebirds in the fall, herons and waterfowl in the spring and fall, nesting Least Terns and Piping Plovers in the summer, and Snow Buntings in the early winter. Park at the end of the boardwalk, cross the marsh, and go right around the point and back along the beach.

Shawme Pond and **Upper Shawme Pond**, in the village center, usually have a good assortment of wintering waterfowl. Among the masses of pan-handling Ring-billed Gulls, Mallards and mixed-breed ducks on Shawme Pond you may find Pied-billed Grebes, Mute Swans, a Wood Duck or two, Ring-necked Ducks, Common Goldeneyes, and coots. At Upper Shawme look for Pied-billed Grebes, Gadwalls, American Wigeon, Ring-necked Ducks, and Common Goldeneyes. The beautiful woodlands and thickets surrounding the ponds can provide some excellent land birding at any

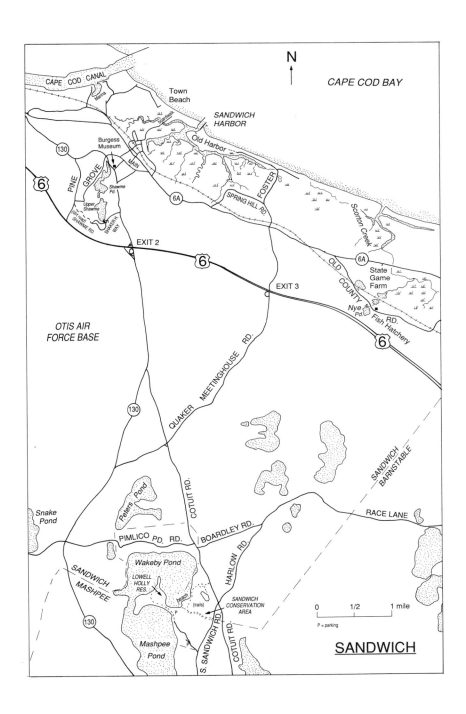

season. Shawme Pond can be checked from the Thornton Burgess Museum on Route 130 and from Grove Street along its western shore. Upper Shawme is accessible from Shaker House Way; watch for a small gazebo where there is room to pull off and park.

The **Old Harbor** area is worth checking for a variety of shorebirds, which sometimes include Whimbrels, Willets, and Pectoral Sandpipers. Great Black-backed and Herring Gulls and Common and Least Terns nest on the point. From the end of Foster Road, turn left, park where the soft sand begins, and walk west out the spit.

The **Fish Hatchery** on Old County Road is among the most productive birding spots in Sandwich. A variety of nesting songbirds can be found including Carolina and House Wrens, Wood Thrushes and in some years Orchard Orioles. Nye Pond, which is across the street from the fish hatchery, should be checked in the colder months for ducks, especially Ring-necked Ducks.

The **Lowell Holly Reservation** (owned by the Trustees of Reservations) and the **Sandwich Conservation Area** are located in South Sandwich and front on Wakeby Pond. The habitat is mostly woodland, composed of white and pitch pines, oaks, hollies, and maples, but there is also an overgrown cranberry bog, a small pond, and good views of Wakeby Pond. Trails through the properties are not always well-marked, but it is difficult to get lost.

Birding can be good at any season, but even if the birds are scarce, the area is wonderful to simply wander through. Breeding birds include Eastern Screech-Owls, Ruffed Grouse, Wood Thrushes, Pine Warblers, Ovenbirds, American Redstarts, and Scarlet Tanagers. During migration, small numbers of migrant warblers may be found. Winter birds often include Red and White-breasted Nuthatches, Brown Creepers, Golden-crowned Kinglets, and robins. On the lake, look for Common Loons, Pied-billed Grebes, and Common Goldeneyes.

There are three entrances to the area. A small dirt parking lot located 3/10 mile north of South Sandwich Road on Cotuit Road leads to the overgrown bog, small pond, and Wakeby Pond. The main entrance to the Sandwich Conservation Area is on South Sandwich Road, 2/10 mile from Cotuit Road, and winds down to a large dirt parking area near the town beach (permit required in summer). This parking area also provides access to both the Lowell Holly Reservation (by walking along the beach) and to trails leading to the small pond and bog. The main entrance to the Lowell Reservation is on South Sandwich Road, 7/10 mile from Cotuit Road, but is not well marked. There is parking space for one or two cars.

MASHPEE

Located on the south shore of Cape Cod, between the towns of Falmouth and Barnstable, Mashpee has pine barrens, mixed pine/oak woodlands, and a fine barrier beach and estuarine river system. Two prime birding areas containing these habitats are South Cape Beach and the Mashpee River.

The **Mashpee River** begins at Mashpee Pond and flows south to Nantucket Sound. Much of the land bordering the river is managed by the Mashpee River Woodlands Committee and the Trustees of Reservations, and encompasses one of the only mature, forested river systems on Cape Cod. Good birding trails are access-ible from the dirt parking area located off Route 28, Quinaquisset Avenue, Mashpee Neck Road, and River Road; trail diagrams and information are posted at various locations. In the breeding season, Broad-winged Hawks, Ospreys, Yellow-billed and Black-billed Cuckoos, Red-breasted Nuthatches, Brown Creepers, Marsh Wrens, Brown Thrashers, Northern Parulas, Pine Warblers, and Swamp Sparrows are among the more notable residents. In other seasons, Common Snipes, Virginia Rails, Winter Wrens, and Golden-crowned and Ruby-crowned Kinglets are often present.

South Cape Beach is a municipally owned barrier beach and marsh that supports many of the birds associated with this habitat. Mute Swans, herons, Ospreys, Roseate and Least Terns, and Sharp-tailed and Seaside Sparrows may be seen during the warmer months. In the marsh and at the end of the beach, check for shore-birds including Piping Plovers, Whimbrels, Spotted Sandpipers and "peeps." Offshore, scan for Horned Grebes, sea ducks, gulls, and terns in season. Along the woodland trails behind the marsh, search for Ruffed Grouse, Great Horned Owls, Whip-poor-wills, and Pine Warblers. A thicket at the end of the barrier beach is a great place to explore in late fall and winter for land birds. During this season, search the surrounding beach for Snow Buntings and the break-water for Purple Sandpipers, which have been seen there on rare occasions.

Washburn Island is an interesting but little-known area to birders and can only be reached by boat or canoe from the boat landings. Flat Pond and Waquoit Bay are worth scanning for some of the more common waterfowl.

John's Pond frequently has wintering Pied-billed Grebes, scaup, Ring-necked Ducks, Common Goldeneyes, Common Mer-gansers, and coots. It is best checked from Back Road on its north shore and James Circle on its south shore.

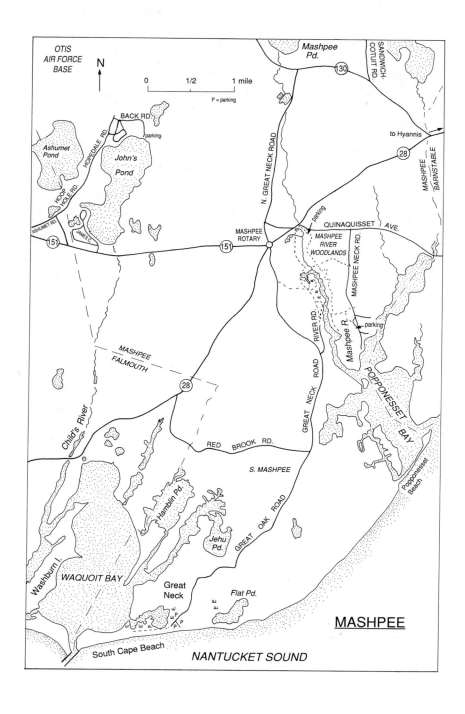

2 THE MID CAPE

The Mid Cape area, as defined here, includes the five towns from Barnstable east to Brewster and Harwich, and offers broad frontage on Cape Cod Bay to the north and Nantucket Sound to the south. It is an area of sharp contrasts, as it contains some of the Cape's most congested and depressing sections, such as Hyannis and the tacky-town sections of Route 28 through Yarmouth and Dennis, as well as some of its most wild and beautiful spots, including such prime birding locations as the magnificent Sandy Neck dune and marsh system in Barnstable; Chapin Beach, Corporation Beach, and West Dennis Beach in Dennis; the West Harwich Conservation Area; Nickerson State Park in Brewster, and a variety of good waterfowl ponds throughout.

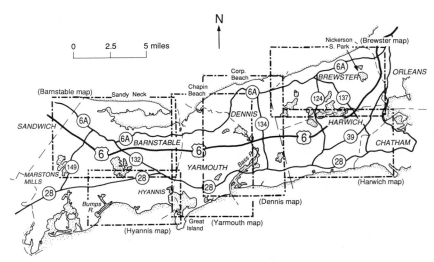

Mid Cape

BARNSTABLE

Barnstable, the largest of the Cape's towns, encompasses over 60 square miles and contains a wide variety of habitats. There is a sharp contrast between the northern half of the town, which somehow has remained fairly quiet, with such wild and relatively undisturbed areas as Sandy Neck and the Marstons Mills woodlands, and the southern half of town, which harbors the congested

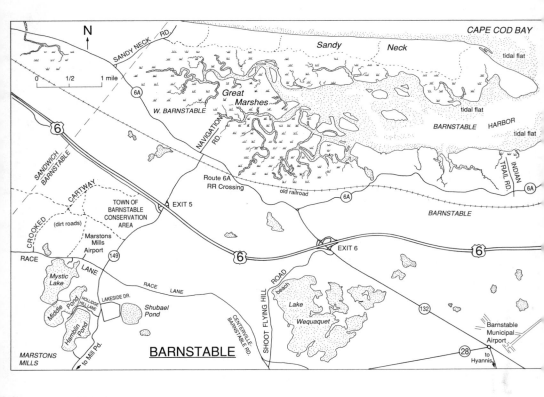

village of Hyannis, the commercial center of Cape Cod, and acre upon acre of densely-packed residential neighborhoods. However, there is good birding throughout the town, and should you find yourself stuck in Hyannis at some time, you needn't despair for there is likely to be a productive spot somewhere nearby.

The **Sandy Neck** parking lot is one of the best places in New England to watch pelagics during a northeaster. For best results, the wind must be blowing at least 25 miles per hour from a northeast direction and should be the result of a storm that has moved up the coast. Anytime from May to December can be a good time to see pelagics, although the fall produces most consistently. Park on the upper lot with the vehicle facing almost into the wind. (If sand is blowing hard, find a way to keep the windshield from being sand-blasted.) Open the windows on the left (west) side and you'll have an unobstructed view of the birds that come along the edge of the water, often within close viewing range. From the relative comfort of your car it is possible to see shearwaters, storm-petrels, phalaropes, kittiwakes, jaegers, and alcids, depending on the season, as well as rarer species such as Northern Fulmar or Little Gull.

Sandy Neck is an expansive barrier beach system containing a surprising array of upland habitats among the dune hollows. Rides down "the Neck" are always an experience but require a four-wheel-drive vehicle and a permit from the town. Walking the entire beach takes considerable stamina, as the trek is six miles each way, mostly through soft sand. The marsh side is closed to vehicles but can often be more interesting than the beach. The clam flats near the point are the best places to look for shorebirds in late summer and fall. Peregrine Falcons are regular fall migrants and are a likely sight from late September to mid-October. The pockets of woodland among the dunes harbor migrant songbirds.

Those hardy enough to find their way out into the Great Marshes of Barnstable, between Sandy Neck and the mainland, will find Sharp-tailed and Seaside Sparrows nesting at the western end of the marsh. The second half of May is the best time to look and listen; the sparrows are claiming their territory then.

Navigation Road, at its end, is a prime spot for watching marsh birds during flood tides in the fall. Look for a tide of 11 feet or more (Boston tide) and park at the end of the road at least 15 minutes before the tide is due to crest in Boston. Sometimes the water covers all of the road so don't get marooned. Shorebirds, herons, and rails get pushed up out of the ditches as the water rises. It can be a thrilling show if you hit it just right.

The **Route 6A Railroad Crossing** in Barnstable has had nesting Willow Flycatchers on the south side of the road for several years. Marsh Wrens linger in the reeds until everything freezes, and Virginia Rails and more rarely Soras linger late enough to be recorded on the Christmas Bird Count.

Indian Trail Road leads to Barnstable Harbor and is worth checking for sea ducks in winter. At low tide you can have fun walking way out into the harbor on exposed mud flats and spits to watch migrant shorebirds, which may include almost any of the typical Northeast species.

The **Town of Barnstable Conservation Area** offers what is probably the greatest variety of nesting land birds to be found on Cape Cod. This area is accessible from Crooked Cartway, which becomes a rough, dirt, woods road, often closed to vehicular traffic but passable on foot. The road leads through many acres of pine/oak woodlands, interspersed with occasional brushy clearings and provides a good opportunity for exploring. Red-tailed Hawks, Ruffed Grouse, Northern Bobwhites, and Great Horned Owls are present throughout the year, and during the nesting season you may find Black-billed and Yellow-billed Cuckoos; Red-breasted and White-breasted Nuthatches; Brown Creepers; Wood Thrushes; and Pine, Prairie, Yellow, Black-and-white, and rarely Blue-winged Warblers; Ovenbirds; Scarlet Tanagers; and Indigo Buntings. In the spring, American Woodcocks perform their courtship displays in the open areas at dusk, and later in the evening, Whip-poor-wills serenade throughout the woodlands.

The **Marstons Mills Airport**, at the intersection of Race Lane and Route 149 is a small, privately owned airfield with grass runways and extensive brushy edges. During the summer, Ring-necked Pheasants, Northern Bobwhites, Black-billed Cuckoos, Brown Thrashers, Prairie and Yellow Warblers, Field Sparrows, and Eastern Meadowlarks are present. Grasshopper Sparrows used to nest here but are seen only rarely now. Woodcocks perform their mating flights in the open areas in the spring; Great Horned Owls hoot from the wooded margins on still evenings; and Whip-poor-wills chorus on summer nights. Rough-legged Hawks have been seen here occasionally during the winter. You can park at the small dirt parking area on the northeast corner of the airport (along Route 149) or at the intersection of Route 149 and Race Lane.

The **Marstons Mills Ponds** are excellent spots to see wintering waterfowl. *Mill Pond*, at the intersection of Route 28 and Route 149 is a picturesque body of water containing an interesting mixture of barnyard ducks. However, be sure to look beyond these ducks to the

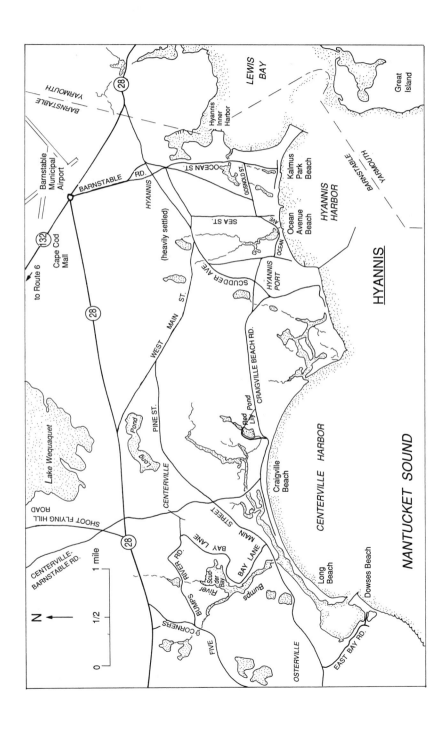

far side of the pond as this is one of the most consistent places on the Cape to find wintering Gadwalls, and occasionally a Wood Duck. *Hamblin Pond*, off Route 149, usually has a good variety of ducks and rarely a white-winged gull. Hollidge Hill Lane, marked private, leads into an area that gives you several vantage points into Hamblin Pond as well as Middle Pond. Considerate birders are welcome. *Shubael Pond*, east off Route 149 on Lakeside Drive, is a good spot for scaup and Ruddy Ducks. *Mystic Lake*, off Race Lane, should be checked from the town landing for Pied-billed Grebes, scaup, Canvasbacks, Common Mergansers, and coots.

Lake Wequaquet is the largest freshwater lake on Cape Cod. In winter, look from the heights above the public beach on Shoot Flying Hill Road for Pied-billed Grebes, Canvasbacks, scaup, Common Mergansers, and other ducks.

Kalmus Park Beach, a small barrier beach at the end of Ocean Street in Hyannis, is an interesting place to spend an early morning hour or two year-round. The evergreens and oaks on the left as you enter the gate are worth a quick prowl to check for a possible Northern Saw-whet Owl in the fall, and landbirds during migration. Phragmites grow on the north side of the parking lot, where a marsh was filled in the late 1950s. In spring and summer, if you walk out to the beach, east behind the beach house to the breakwater, you may see Horned Larks and usually Least Terns and Piping Plovers. In winter you can often see Snow Buntings, many Oldsquaws and other sea ducks, and rarely a Short-eared Owl. The point of land across the channel to the east is Great Island, once the home of C. B. Cory, the turn-of-the-century field ornithologist/naturalist for whom the Cory's Shearwater is named. His home was a gathering spot for collectors, hunters, and naturalists.

Ocean Avenue (Sea Street) beach and marsh, between Hyannis and Hyannisport, is worth more than a casual look throughout the year. Parking in the off-season or early morning is available in the Sea Street Beach parking lot. Walk up the small bluff to the east to scan the water for loons, grebes, Brant, eiders, goldeneyes (occasionally including a Barrow's), and Oldsquaws in winter, and in summer for gulls and terns. Then walk down the beach to the west to check the area where the creek flows under the road. The tidal marsh on the north side of the road has entertained, in proper seasons, night-herons, teal, Northern Pintail, shorebirds, coots, and Hooded, Common and Red-breasted Mergansers.

The **Craigville Beach area** contains the recently reclaimed Red Lily Pond by the Craigville Conference Center, which can host a few ducks during the fall and winter, including Pied-billed Grebes and

Ring-necked Ducks. From the west end of the Craigville Beach parking lots, you can walk to the west out Long Beach. Near its western point this barrier beach has a Common Tern nesting colony and usually a pair or two of Piping Plovers. Please be careful not to disturb the birds when approaching the nesting areas.

Scudder Bay-Bumps River, a good area year-round, is best at low tide when the flats host feeding shorebirds, gulls, herons, and puddle ducks. During past winters, this has been a reliable place to find Green-winged Teal and American Wigeon. Northern Parulas have nested for the last few years on the northwest side of the bay, as well as where Bumps River goes under Five Corners Road. Most of the property along the river and bay is privately owned, but several spots along Bay Lane have openings that permit a view of the water and flats.

Dowses Beach in Osterville provides a good view of Nantucket Sound, where wintering Horned Grebes, loons, Common Golden-eyes, scoters, and eiders are usually present. In summer, from the east end of the parking lot, you can look across to Long Beach to see the nesting Common Terns. Check carefully as Roseate Terns have been seen here frequently.

YARMOUTH

Bounded by Cape Cod Bay to the north and Nantucket Sound to the south, Yarmouth offers a variety of birding habitats that include salt marshes, freshwater ponds, overgrown bogs, and wooded areas.

Hallet's Mill Pond is the best place on the Cape for Northern Pintail in winter, and a variety of other ducks are usually present as well. During the warmer months look for herons, shorebirds, and terns at low tide. Just to the east, off Water Street, a short dirt road leads out to the marshes and the mouth of Barnstable Harbor. This is an excellent place to view waterfowl and shorebirds.

Bass Hole (Gray's Beach) has a long boardwalk out across the marsh from which you can see herons, shorebirds, and occasionally a rail. At the end look far to the west to the sandy dune at the water's edge. During the breeding season this area teems with nesting Common Terns, and usually a few Roseate Terns. Willets and nesting Piping Plovers may also be found, and, if you're lucky, you may see an American Oystercatcher, Black Tern, or Black Skimmer. The berry bushes on the picnic grounds are attractive to migratory and nesting passerines. In fall and winter the boardwalk affords an excellent vantage point to view geese, sea ducks, and gulls. In winter

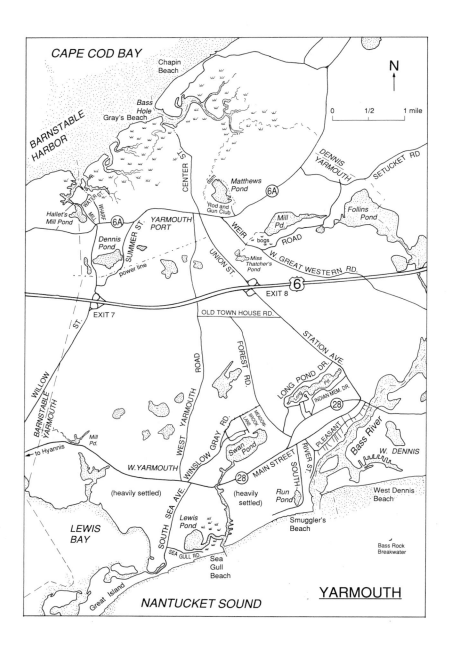

CAPE COD BAY

Chapin
Beach

N

0   1/2   1 mile

BARNSTABLE
HARBOR

Bass
Hole
Gray's Beach

Matthews
Pond

DENNIS
YARMOUTH

SETUCKET RD.

CENTER ST.

6A

WATER ST.

WHARF

Hallet's
Mill Pond

MILL

6A

Rod and
Gun Club

YARMOUTH
PORT

WEIR

Mill
Pd.

bogs

ROAD

Follins
Pond

Dennis
Pond

SUMMER ST.

power line

UNION ST.

Miss
Thatcher's
Pond

W. GREAT WESTERN RD.

6

EXIT 8

EXIT 7

OLD TOWN HOUSE RD.

STATION AVE.

WILLOW ST.

BARNSTABLE
YARMOUTH

to Hyannis

Mill
Pd.

FOREST RD.

WEST YARMOUTH ROAD

LONG POND DR.

Long
Pd.

INDIAN MEM. DR.

28

WINSLOW GRAY RD.

MEADOW
BROOK
LANE

Swan
Pond

28

MAIN STREET

PLEASANT

RIVER ST.

Bass River

W. DENNIS

W. YARMOUTH

(heavily settled)

(heavily
settled)

Run
Pond

SOUTH

West Dennis
Beach

SOUTH SEA AVE.

LEWIS
BAY

Lewis
Pond

SEA GULL RD.

Sea
Gull
Beach

Smuggler's
Beach

Bass Rock
Breakwater

Great Island

NANTUCKET SOUND

YARMOUTH

Horned Larks, Snow Buntings, and rarely a Short-eared Owl have been seen around the parking lot.

Dennis Pond is an area where, with luck, you can encounter migrating warblers and other passerines in May. Do your birding by walking west along the railroad tracks or east on a path parallel to the tracks. You might also walk along Summer Street. Follow the road past the beach to the power lines. Look for hawks on the lines (Broad-winged Hawks nest in the area) and nesting House Wrens, Prairie Warblers, and Field Sparrows along the paths.

The **Bass River Rod and Gun Club** welcomes birders; hunting is *not* allowed. Park at the clubhouse and do your birding from the platform overlooking Tom Matthews Pond. During fall, mild winters, and early spring, Wood Ducks, Green-winged and Blue-winged Teals, Canvasbacks, rarely Redheads, Ring-necked Ducks, Buffle-heads, Hooded and Common Mergansers, and Ruddy Ducks can be seen. Great Blue Herons roost in the trees across the pond, and Rough-winged Swallows have nested on the property. If you walk down the dirt road bordering the pond on the right, which leads to the dam, you may see woodpeckers, warblers, and an occasional hawk or owl. River Otters, which are very rare on Cape Cod, have been seen in the pond.

The **Weir Road** area, with its abandoned cranberry bogs, deciduous woodlands, and Miss Thatcher's and Mill ponds, offers a good variety of resident and migrant passerines, hawks, and waterfowl. During April and May, American Woodcocks perform their mating ceremonies in some of the open areas. Look for the Osprey pole on the edge of Mill Pond. In May, birders have a good chance of running into an early morning warbler wave along Weir Road or Great Western Road which branches off to the right. One resident has recorded more than 150 species in the neighborhood.

Long Pond generally has wintering Canvasbacks, Ring-necked Ducks, scaup, Common Goldeneyes, and Buffleheads. The pond can be viewed from vantage points along Indian Memorial Drive, Lakeland Avenue, Ice House Road, and Long Pond Drive.

The **Bass River** is a good spot to see shorebirds and terns in season, as well as wintering loons, cormorants, Common Eiders, goldeneyes (including an occasional Barrow's) Buffleheads, Red-breasted Mergansers, and gulls. The parking lot at Smuggler's Beach offers good views of the mouth of the river and Nantucket Sound, and you can find other vantage points by the windmill parking lot off River Street and various side roads off Pleasant Street. Run Pond, across the street from the Smuggler's Beach parking lot, is a good area in spring for viewing Snowy and Great Egrets and Rough-winged Swallows.

Sea Gull Beach has several marshy areas, on the right as you enter, that may have egrets, shorebirds, and rarely a rail. Lewis Pond and the salt marsh on the left host shorebirds and waders and are good for Whimbrels during August, especially in the evening. American Kestrels and Northern Harriers occur throughout most of the year. The old Christmas trees placed along the parking lot are a good place to look for sparrows.

Swan Pond is an excellent area to look for wintering Canvasbacks and scaup, which can be seen well from a boardwalk at the extreme end of Meadowbrook Lane.

Baxter Mill Pond abuts a small park on busy Route 28. The pond is worth checking for winter ducks, including Gadwalls, American Wigeon and Ring-necked Ducks as well as Pied-billed Grebes and Common Snipes. The adjacent thickets attract a few migratory and nesting landbirds.

DENNIS

Straddling the mid-Cape area is the town of Dennis which extends from Cape Cod Bay on the north to Nantucket Sound on the south.

Dennis has some fine birding spots on both coasts as well as freshwater ponds that attract wintering waterfowl.

Chapin Beach offers birders the chance to see various sea and bay birds, and at low tide, extensive flats are exposed, which can attract migrant shorebirds. In winter the salt marshes and dunes have hosted Short-eared Owls and Snow Buntings.

Corporation Beach, three miles east of Chapin Beach, can provide excellent birding for loons, grebes, sea ducks, gulls, and alcids in season. If the weather is foul, often the best conditions for birding here, you may want to watch from your car. In the fall and early winter during and immediately following a northeaster, hundreds of gannets, as well as many other seabirds, may pass by, often at very close range. In spring this is a principal gathering place for migrating Red-necked Grebes, counts of which often exceed 100 birds.

Swan Pond and **Swan River** are excellent spots to see wintering Canvasbacks, scaup, and Common Mergansers. There is often open water here when all else has frozen. Good vantage points are available from the river overpass on Upper County Road, from Indian Trail and Clipper Lane off Upper County Road, and from Vester Drive off Depot Street. A small park, "Swan Pond Overlook" on Center Street between Searsville Road and Depot Street, has trails and an excellent view of the pond.

West Dennis Beach, a barrier beach with a wide variety of habitats, is worth visiting in all seasons. Approaching from School Street, turn right at the triangle where a pine grove which has occasionally harbored a roosting Short-eared Owl in winter, stands. Continuing on to the beach parking area, a salt marsh borders a tidal creek on your right and Nantucket Sound, sandy beach, and a ridge of small dunes are on your left. Out in the sound a rocky breakwater is a favorite year-round roost for cormorants and gulls. The beach road ends at Bass River which, in winter, is a haven for geese and ducks, including Barrow's Goldeneye in some years; in summer the river is a feeding place for shorebirds and terns at low tide. Least Terns, Horned Larks, and Savannah Sparrows nest in the dunes, and Common Terns nest in the sandy areas between the river and the marsh. In the marsh, herons, egrets, a variety of shorebirds (including Whimbrel), and Sharp-tailed Sparrows may be found. You may see rails in the marsh in fall and early winter, and Horned Larks and Snow Buntings throughout the colder months.

Cove Road, going north from Route 28, offers two good areas for viewing winter waterfowl. At the end of the road is a large parking lot with an excellent view of Bass River and Grand Cove. Aunt Julia

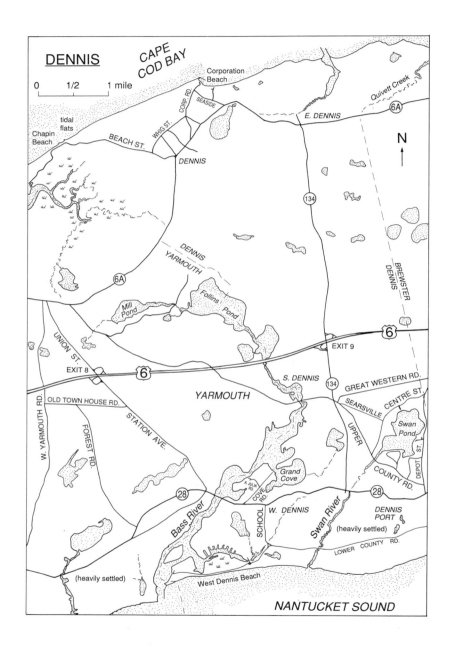

Ann Road, on the right as you return to Route 28, leads to a landing where there is almost always open water in the winter. Canada Geese, Buffleheads, goldeneyes and others are typically present.

BREWSTER

In the mid-Cape area, Brewster extends from Cape Cod Bay south to the town of Harwich. Although it is one of the least developed towns on the Cape, Brewster is also one of the fastest growing. Brewster has been zoned for larger lot sizes, and numerous conservation areas are being protected, so many productive birdwatching sites may remain available for future generations to enjoy. Prime birding attractions include a number of freshwater ponds, several vantages to Cape Cod Bay, and extensive pine/oak woodlands.

Paine's Creek Beach is a good location from which birders can observe Paine's Creek, the adjoining marsh, and Cape Cod Bay. During fall storms, with winds out of the north, you may witness a good pelagic show from this vantage point, but you need to be present during high tide or the birds will be too far out to be readily identified. In August and September a wide assortment of shorebirds can be seen on the extensive mud flats during low tide. Caution: you can walk for a mile or more out into the bay during low tide

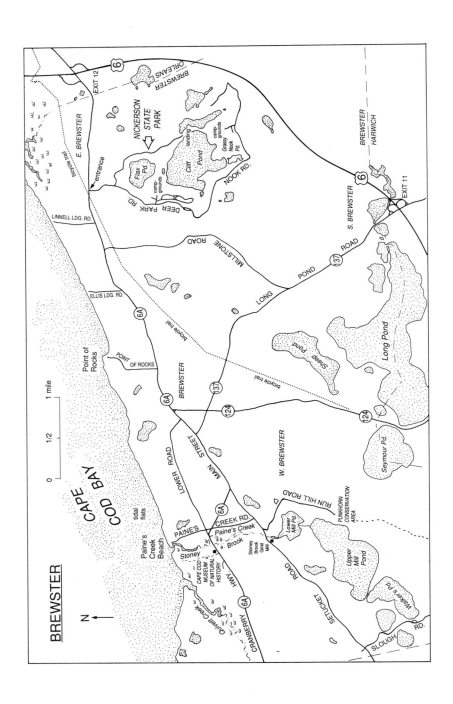

but you must watch carefully for the turning tide in order to make it to shore safely. Almost every year some unsuspecting person has to be rescued.

Nickerson State Park covers more than 1,750 acres and includes a public campground with over 400 sites that operates on a first-come, first-served basis and is usually full during peak summer months. The park includes five clear, freshwater ponds, four of which have good trout fishing. The park proper has 7½ miles of bicycle trails that connect to over 30 miles of the Cape Cod Rail Trail which runs from Dennis through Eastham. Birding by bicycle in this area can be an interesting experience. At Nickerson, impressive numbers of migrant and wintering waterfowl can be found; Common Mergansers can be especially numerous in early winter, and other species may include Pied-billed Grebes, large numbers of Black Ducks, Ring-necked Ducks, Common Goldeneyes, Hooded Mergansers, and Ruddy Ducks. The smaller, more secluded ponds often have Wood Ducks during migration. Another feature of the park is its consistency in producing owls for those who enjoy listening for the nocturnal calls of these shy residents. Great Horned and Eastern Screech-Owls are relatively common, Northern Saw-whet Owls less common but heard with some regularity. Late winter to early spring is the most productive time, but you must pick a night with little or no wind for the best results. Nesting species in the park include Red-tailed Hawk, Ruffed Grouse, Whip-poor-will, Hairy Woodpecker, Red-breasted and White-breasted Nuthatches, Brown Creeper, Wood Thrush, Ovenbird, Black-and-white and Pine Warblers, Scarlet Tanager, and Purple Finch.

Point of Rocks is an excellent vantage point for Cape Cod Bay. During the summer months birders are often rewarded with views of shorebirds, and in the fall, migrating sea birds including pelagics can be seen if conditions are right. Impressive numbers of Brant may be present in November and December. Other good views of the bay can be had from the ends of Ellis Landing Road and Linnell Landing Road.

Upper Mill Pond and **Lower Mill Pond** are the destination of thousands of Atlantic Herring, or Alewife, that migrate each spring from the Atlantic Ocean up Paine's Creek to the Stoney Brook herring run. The ponds are located south of the Stoney Brook Grist Mill, which is a popular visitor attraction. If you stop at various vantage points off Run Hill Road, you can often find Pied-billed Grebes, Canvasbacks, Ring-necked Ducks, scaup, Common Goldeneyes, Common and Hooded Mergansers, and American Coots.

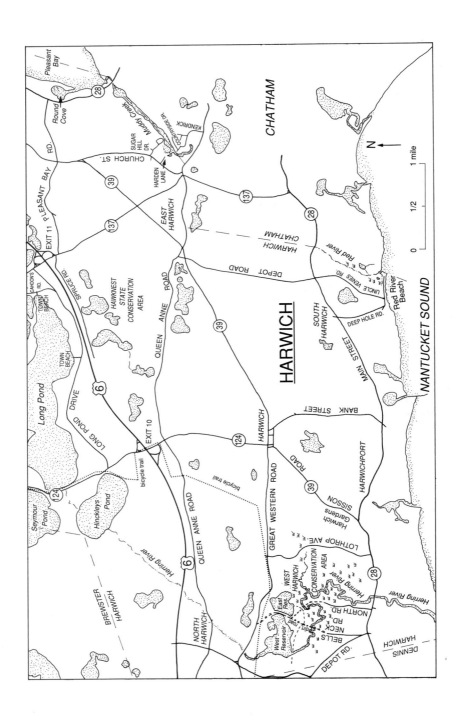

Walker's Pond has traditionally been a favorite spot for wintering waterfowl including Pied-billed Grebes, Canvasbacks, Ring-necked Ducks, scaup, Common Mergansers, and American Coots. The boat launching area on Slough Road offers a good place to view the pond.

The **Cape Cod Museum of Natural History**, located on Route 6A, is a good rainy-day destination for any naturalist. The museum has an impressive natural history library with a wide assortment of quality bird books. In addition to the library, the museum has many programs, natural history displays, a gift shop, and outdoor trails through a variety of typical Cape Cod habitats. Also, the Cape Cod Bird Club meets at the museum at 7:45 p.m. on the second Monday of each month from September through June. This museum is a real gem and well worth a stop.

HARWICH

Located in the mid-Cape region, Harwich extends from Nantucket Sound in the south to the town of Brewster in the north. Numerous freshwater ponds, most the result of glacial deposits, are typically surrounded by upland forest with oaks dominating and pines taking a secondary role in the forest canopy. Primary birding attractions include several ponds, which host a good variety of wintering diving ducks, and the extensive conservation area in the southwest corner of town, which is the site of one of the largest expanses of freshwater marsh on Cape Cod.

The **West Harwich Conservation Area** on Bells Neck Road in West Harwich was designated to protect the Herring River watershed. A unique area by local standards, this conservation area offers an "almost-wilderness" experience in the middle of all the hustle and bustle of Cape Cod. The best place to start birding is between the East and West reservoirs on Bells Neck Road (park on the side of the road). The East Reservoir has been shallow and brackish ever since a dike separating the reservoir from the marsh broke open a few years ago, whereas the West Reservoir is deep and fresh, thereby affecting which species are seen. Birding is good during any season, but in late summer the vegetation around the East Reservoir grows very thick, making it difficult to get a decent view. During the summer and early fall, scan the mud flats in the middle of the East Reservoir for shorebirds, herons, and Least Terns that gather here. During migration this is a good spot for puddle ducks, particularly teal, Gadwalls, and American Wigeon. Virginia

Rails have nested in the cattails along the edges of the reservoir and are regularly heard in the fall and early winter.

Check the dead trees in the West Reservoir and along the edges of the water for Ospreys, which often frequent this area; Double-crested Cormorants; night-herons; and if you are very lucky, a Bald Eagle. Pied-billed Grebes and a few diving ducks can often be found here from September through April. Great Horned Owls reside throughout the wooded sections of this still-wild area.

Continuing south on Bells Neck Road, you will reach the Herring River and a large marsh that can be scanned from the bridge. This point is an ideal area to watch and listen for nesting Marsh Wrens, Swamp Sparrows, and occasionally Virginia Rails and Least Bitterns. Northern Parulas have nested along the wooded edges; notice the beard moss, which is used by these warblers in their nests, growing on the dead trees. During migration Virginia Rails and Soras can be quite common, and raptors such as Ospreys, Northern Harriers, or Red-tailed Hawks may be seen.

From here you can either take the trail easterly through the woods along the north edge of the marsh or retrace your steps back along the road and take a right on North Road. Both will bring you to the North Road footbridge, which offers another lookout over the marsh which is more brackish here. Just before the footbridge an old dirt road runs north along the west edge of the marsh, ending in a small clearing. From there, a narrow, overgrown path leads north-easterly through the phragmites and poison ivy to a small wooded island which is a good vantage point for the other side of the East Reservoir and marsh. This island often has a variety of landbirds, especially warblers, particularly during spring migration.

If you are interested in aquatic plants, the West Reservoir is a fascinating area, one that is best explored by canoe. You will be amazed at how close you can approach birds and other forms of wildlife in a canoe. This locale is an unusual example of a freshwater habitat in an area generally known only for coastal beaches, dunes, and marshes.

The **Harwich Gardens**, on Route 124/39 (Sisson Road), are on town conservation land that is set aside for residents to garden. The area is productive for fall migrant sparrows, Bobolinks, Indigo Buntings, and rarer species such as Blue Grosbeaks and Dickcissels.

Red River Beach is a town-owned barrier beach and a good vantage point for the Red River Marsh to the north of the parking lot and Nantucket Sound to the south. Red River separates the towns of Harwich and Chatham and provides some nice habitat for a few herons, shorebirds, and other marsh birds. This beach can be very

crowded during the summer season, but after prime beach time or during the off-season it provides some decent birding. This portion of Nantucket Sound often has many sea ducks, terns, gulls. Both King Eider and Barrow's Goldeneye have been seen here.

Muddy Creek on the Harwich-Chatham border is a small but productive area especially worth checking in the winter when every-thing else is frozen. Because of numerous springs, this area tends to stay open even during the coldest of seasons. One of the most productive portions of the creek is located at the end of Harden Lane. Along the edge — be careful, this area is a quagmire, and you can sink to your knees quickly — you may find wintering Common Snipes, an American Woodcock or a Virginia Rail, and herons. In the open water many waterfowl winter, often including Green-winged Teal, Northern Pintail, American Wigeon, Hooded and Common Mergansers, and sometimes a Wood Duck. Wintering landbirds are numerous in the surrounding thickets and at the many feeders in the neighborhood. Additional views of the creek are available from Sugar Hill Drive just to the north, and from Queen Anne Road and Countryside Drive on the other side of the creek in Chatham.

Round Cove is the geographical center of the Cape Cod Christmas Bird Count. This protected cove is worth a quick check during the winter months when Mute Swans, Brant, a few puddle ducks, and a lingering heron or shorebird are possible.

Long Pond, Hinckleys Pond, and **Seymour Pond** feature wintering diving duck populations. Waterfowl that can be expected include Pied-billed Grebes, Canvasbacks, Ring-necked Ducks, scaup, Common Goldeneyes, Common Mergansers, Ruddy Ducks, and American Coots. The three ponds in this area are all accessible from Route 124; it is possible to view most of the ponds from just a few vantage points. Check Hinckleys from below the small parking lot across from the Pleasant Lake General Store, Long Pond from where the bicycle path crosses Route 124, and Seymour from a small dirt parking lot 9/10 of a mile beyond the general store. The eastern portions of Long Pond can be checked from town beaches off Long Pond Drive and Cahoon's Road.

The **Hawknest State Conservation Area** is largely undeveloped and not easily accessible. This large tract of pine/oak woodland with three good-sized ponds holds a variety of birding opportunities but has not had the coverage that it probably deserves. Hawknest is a good area for Great Horned Owls, Eastern Screech-Owls and Whip-poor-wills. The state is considering making this area an extension of Nickerson State Park thus affording birders the opportunity for more extensive exploration. The best access at present is from Spruce Road off of Route 137.

3 THE OUTER CAPE

The Outer Cape, from the "elbow" at Chatham to the "clenched fist" of Provincetown, offers some of the top birding sites anywhere in New England. If your time is limited, plan to spend most or all of it in this area. Good birding spots abound, but some of the more prominent are: Morris Island in Chatham; Nauset Beach in Orleans; Fort Hill, First Encounter Beach, and Coast Guard Beach in Eastham; the Wellfleet Bay Wildlife Sanctuary in South Wellfleet; the Pilgrim Heights area in Truro; and the Beech Forest and Race Point area of Provincetown. It is a rare day, indeed, that fails to produce something of interest in one or more of these areas.

CHATHAM

At the "elbow" of Cape Cod, Chatham offers the charm of a rural seaside village combined with some superb birding possibilities. Chatham often leaves the first-time visitor with the impression of a liquid landscape, as the town is bordered on three sides by water and is pocketed by numerous bays, inlets, and ponds. The vast expanses of water and extensive shoreline attract large numbers of migrant shorebirds and wintering waterfowl. During the fall migration, southbound passerines and raptors become botttlenecked here, and when the winds are northwesterly, impressive concentrations can result. In the winter the numerous thickets and residential plantings provide berries and shelter for a variety of lingering species that are rare on the mainland of Massachusetts in this season.

Forest Beach is a small barrier beach and salt marsh on Nantucket Sound, which is worth checking in the winter for sea ducks. During the warmer months look for herons, a few shorebirds, particularly Whimbrels in late summer, and nesting Sharp-tailed Sparrows. Barrow's Goldeneye, King Eider, and the Harlequin have all been seen here, though all are very rare. Raptors sometimes use the radio towers as perches and Ospreys recently have begun nesting on one of the poles.

Cockle Cove is another small barrier beach and salt marsh system on Nantucket Sound, which, like Forest Beach, has wintering sea ducks and a few migrant shorebirds and herons.

Ridgevale (Buck's Creek) is a small, shallow estuary that is primarily of interest in the spring when it attracts herons and shorebirds, particularly yellowlegs and Willets. The estuary is usually less productive during the summer and fall. The best time to bird is at low

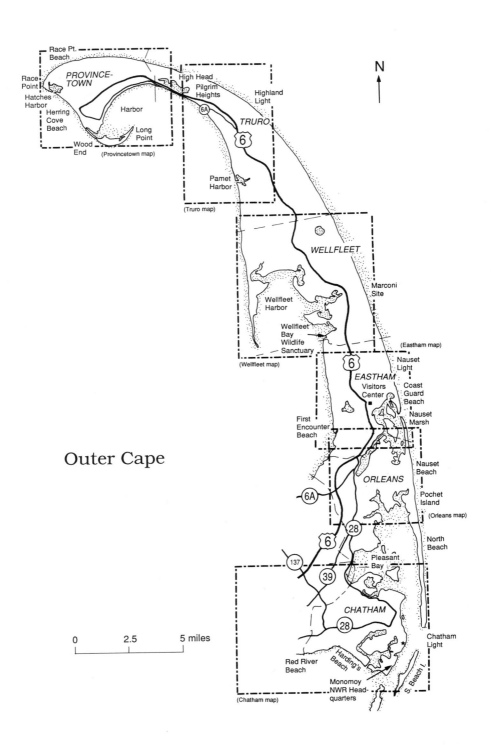

N

PROVINCE-TOWN

Race Pt. Beach

Race Point

Hatches Harbor

Herring Cove Beach

Harbor

Wood End

Long Point

(Provincetown map)

High Head

Pilgrim Heights

Highland Light

6A

TRURO

6

Pamet Harbor

(Truro map)

WELLFLEET

Marconi Site

Wellfleet Harbor

Wellfleet Bay Wildlife Sanctuary

(Wellfleet map)

(Eastham map)

Nauset Light

6

EASTHAM

Visitors Center

Coast Guard Beach

Nauset Marsh

First Encounter Beach

Nauset Beach

Outer Cape

ORLEANS

6A

Pochet Island

(Orleans map)

28

6

North Beach

137

Pleasant Bay

39

CHATHAM

28

Chatham Light

Harding's Beach

0   2.5   5 miles

Red River Beach

Monomoy NWR Head-quarters

S. Beach I.

(Chatham map)

tide, which is approximately three hours after Boston low tide, when the flats are exposed. During higher tides look for herons and roosting shorebirds in the marsh on the south side of the road. For the best vantage, park along the side of the road near the beginning of Ridgevale Road South and walk to the end of the road and out onto the small rise that extends into the marsh.

Harding's Beach is a lovely 1¼-mile barrier beach on Nantucket Sound backed by a narrow yet rather productive salt marsh. If you walk down the beach during the winter, you will often see Northern Harriers, Snow Buntings, Horned Larks, occasionally a Lapland Longspur or an "Ipswich" Sparrow, and rarely a Barrow's Goldeneye, Common Black-headed Gull, Short-eared Owl, or Snowy Owl. During the warmer months watch in the marsh and at the end of the beach for shorebirds as well as herons, terns, and nesting Sharp-tailed and rarely Seaside Sparrows. Piping Plovers and Willets nest here, and American Oystercatchers can often be found on the small flats at the entrance to Oyster River. Access is by foot from the public parking lot.

Stage Harbor, particularly the outer portion, generally has a good assortment of wintering bay ducks, which often includes a Barrow's Goldeneye, and in late fall, terns and small gulls, which

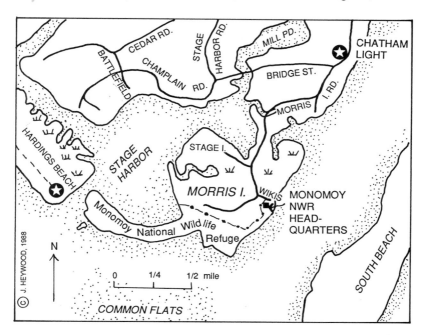

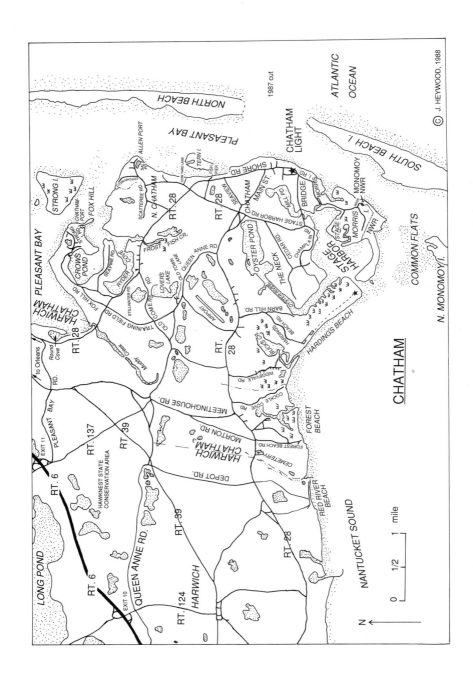

CHATHAM

rarely include a Common Black-headed or Little Gull. The best vantage point is from the town landing on Battlefield Road where the light is best in the afternoon. For those willing to hike a bit, other good vantage points are from the end of Harding's Beach or the end of the beach on Morris Island. A couple of spots along Champlain Road offer less desirable views.

Morris Island, a small oasis in the farthest corner of Chatham, offers some of the finest year-round birding on Cape Cod. A large number and variety of birds are usually present on this island in any season. Although most of Morris Island and all of the adjacent Stage Island are privately owned and generally off-limits to visitors, the federal government owns approximately 56 acres on the east and south sides of Morris Island, which is part of the Monomoy National Wildlife Refuge, so public access is permitted in that portion.

When proceeding out Morris Island Road on the causeway, check both sides of the road for egrets, herons, shorebirds, Common and Least Terns, and small gulls in season. Falcons, accipiters, and Northern Harriers are frequently seen here during migration and winter, and on occasion, a wintering Short-eared Owl courses the marsh at dusk. In the fall watch for kingbirds on the wires and sparrows in the grass. Small numbers of wintering bay ducks can be seen in Stage Harbor on the west side of the causeway.

At the end of the causeway, Stage Island Road on the right leads out to Stage Island. Formerly one of the premier land bird "traps" in New England, this small island has suffered heavy residential development, and the resulting loss of habitat and increasingly restricted access has eliminated the birding prospects here—a particularly sad example of what has happened in many portions of Cape Cod.

Continuing past Stage Island Road, Morris Island Road leads up onto Morris Island. (Do not be intimidated by the "Residents Only" sign.) The roads on the island are all private with restricted access, but visitors are permitted as far as the first road on the left, Wikis Way, which ends shortly at the Monomoy National Wildlife Refuge headquarters where limited public parking is available. The parking lot is very small and fills up early in the day during the summer. If the lot is full, return to the causeway, park on the east side of the road, and either walk back the main road up to the head-quarters or walk the sand trail that leads east from the end of the causeway to the beach. Only limited public exhibits and facilities are present at the headquarters, but pamphlets, including a bird list, are available.

The headquarters lawn offers a spectacular panorama of the Chatham mainland to the north and South Beach and the Atlantic Ocean to the east. Sharp-eyed observers can scope the distant flats on South Beach where it is often possible to pick out the larger, more conspicuous shorebirds, terns, gulls and other waterfowl, and occasional seabirds, especially Northern Gannets, over the ocean beyond. During migration watch for hawks and swallows overhead and over the marsh to the north. Belted Kingfishers and Rough-winged Swallows often nest in the cliff face below.

From behind the headquarters take the trail leading down the stairs and follow the beach to the south end of the island. Monomoy Island beckons from across the deceptively narrow channel to the south (so near, yet so far!), and South Beach island lies to the east. During low tide the mud flats here often attract a variety of shore-birds, which in turn attract migrating Merlins, Peregrine Falcons, Sharp-shinned Hawks, and Northern Harriers. The mussel beds are particularly favored by American Oystercatchers, Willets, and Red Knots from spring through early fall and by Common Eiders and Brant during the winter. Hudsonian and Marbled Godwits are some-times seen here or feeding in the distance on the north end of Monomoy. From mid-May to late September, Common and Least Terns often fish the channels, and during the late summer, they are usually joined by a few Roseate Terns. Double-crested Cormorants are routinely sighted from early spring through the fall and are replaced by Great Cormorants during the winter.

Continuing west along the beach, watch for nesting Piping Plovers and Horned Larks in the summer and Snow Buntings and an occasional Lapland Longspur in the winter. The beach eventually ends at the mouth of Stage Harbor where you can find a few shorebirds and terns in the summer and fall and various small gulls during the late fall and early winter. This is also a good spot from which to check for wintering ducks in Stage Harbor.

South Beach Island was created in January 1987 when a severe winter storm broke through North Beach directly east of Chatham Light. The resulting three-mile long island, now free of vehicle traffic, attracts numerous boaters during the summer, but for most of the year is largely undisturbed and pristine.

Most of the island is composed of dune habitats with limited birding potential. However, the spit on the northwest corner of the island, when not overrun with sunbathers, attracts roosting flocks of cormorants, gulls, and terns in season. Halfway down the west side of the island an area of mud flats is exposed during the lower half of the tidal cycle and attracts a good variety of shorebirds, often including Hudsonian Godwits. The best birding is on the expanding southern tip of the island where large numbers of shorebirds, gulls, and terns roost at high tide. Many birds fly over from North Monomoy to roost here; Hudsonian Godwits, Red Knots, Black-bellied and Semipalmated Plovers, and others can be numerous.

Piping Plovers nest on the island and during August and September small groups of migrants, typically 5 to 15 birds, can be found. Least Terns also frequently nest on the island. During the early summer the flocks of roosting terns will often contain a few Arctic Terns, and during the late summer, Roseate Terns, often numbering into the many hundreds, are present, particularly late in the day. Northern Harriers regularly course the dunes at most any season, and may someday nest on the island now that human disturbance has been reduced. During the fall, Peregrine Falcons and Merlins pass through, wreaking havoc among the remaining shorebirds.

The island is, of course, accessible only by boat. The Wellfleet Bay Wildlife Sanctuary offers guided tours several times a year; call them for details (508-349-2615). Ferry services to the island are available from Outermost Harbor Marine (508-945-2030) and John McGrath (508-945-9378). The ambitious birder can launch a canoe from Morris Island — it's a fairly safe trip if there is little wind, but be sure to get the latest weather forecast before embarking! Scientists studying the area predict that the northern end of the island will gradually erode southward over the next few decades, while the southern end expands, eventually connecting to North Monomoy. Local birders are watching this geological metamorphosis with great interest, eager to see how the area's abundant avifauna adapts to the changes in this dynamic corner of the world.

Chatham Light is a beautiful, well-known vantage point that overlooks the lower portion of Pleasant Bay, the newly formed inlet separating the long, slender spits of North Beach and South Beach, and the Atlantic Ocean beyond. Check the bay for gulls at any season, terns during the warmer months, and waterfowl in the winter. Large flocks of Common Eiders are present here some years. During the early spring and again in the fall, gannets can often be spotted, at times in spectacular concentrations, fishing off the outer beach or in the inlet itself. Parasitic Jaegers will at times wander into the inlet to harass the feeding terns and on rare occasions, a sharp-eyed observer can pick out a few shearwaters plying the distant horizon.

The **Chatham Fish Pier** is worth a quick check in the winter for waterfowl and gulls, including an occasional Iceland or Glaucous Gull. The small island directly across from the pier is Tern Island, once the site of a large tern colony until an invasion of rats drove them out.

North Chatham is a quiet neighborhood of lovely waterfront homes, which offers several vantage points on Pleasant Bay: the Cow Yard, the end of Scatteree Road, and the end of Cotchpinicut Road. Each is worth checking during the winter for Great Cormorants, Brant, Common Eiders, goldeneyes including Barrow's, and other waterfowl. The flats off the Cow Yard attract a few shorebirds during migration. A number of small thickets are scattered throughout this neighborhood and "pishing" at any likely looking spot will often produce a few migrant passerines in the fall or lingering "halfhardies" in the winter.

Frost Fish Creek, a small tidal creek that crosses under Route 28, is often worth a quick look during the winter. The flock of domestic Mallards and halfbreeds on the east side of the road sometimes attracts a wayward Wood Duck, Green-winged Teal, Northern Pintail, or American Wigeon during a winter freeze-up.

Chathamport has extensive waterfront on Pleasant Bay. The end of Strong Island Road is an excellent spot for looking over the bay. A good variety of bay ducks can be found here in the winter, and this is one of the most reliable places on the Cape to find a Barrow's Goldeneye or two. Check over the islands in the bay for hunting Red-tailed Hawks, Northern Harriers, and rarely a Rough-legged Hawk or Bald Eagle.

Crow's Pond is another good spot to look for a Barrow's Goldeneye and other bay ducks during the winter. You can check the pond from Sea Pine Road or the town landing on Fox Hill Road.

Lover's Lake and **Stillwater Pond** attract a variety of pond ducks during the winter; Lover's Lake generally has more birds and is the easier to check of the two ponds. Pied-billed Grebes, Canvasbacks, Ring-necked Ducks, scaup, and American Coots can usually be found, and a Eurasian Wigeon has been present in some winters. Lover's Lake can be checked best from the end of Old Town Lane, a private way whose owners have been tolerant of birders. Stillwater Pond can be seen only from a dangerous curve on Old Comer's Road.

ORLEANS

The town of Orleans, "the gateway to the lower Cape," has become a very busy spot, but it still offers some little-trampled areas for good fall, winter, and spring birding. Because of its location on the Sandwich Moraine, the "backbone" of the Cape, Orleans is characterized by knob and kettle topography including kettle ponds, upland woods, and salt marshes.

Town Cove is a fine birding spot from late fall through early spring. A number of wintering waterfowl can be expected, typically including Great Cormorants, Brant, Black Ducks, Common Goldeneyes, rarely a Barrow's Goldeneye, Buffleheads, and Red-breasted Mergansers. Small numbers of Hooded and Common Mergansers are often present when freshwater ponds have frozen. Great Blue Herons can be seen along the shore year-round and other heron species may be present during the warmer months.

One of the best locations for checking the cove is the Orleans Yacht Club at the end of Cove Road. The west edge of the cove here contains numerous springs that remain open through the most severe cold, attracting wintering Common Snipe, Killdeer, occasionally other shorebirds, and a variety of waterfowl. The small salt marsh behind the parking lot can be productive also; check the trees along the edge for sitting raptors. Other good vantage points for Town Cove include the parking lot behind the Goose Hummock Shop on Route 6A and Asa's Landing off Gibson Road.

The end of **Tonset Road** provides a good outlook over the southern edge of Nauset marsh and bay. During the warmer months, expect to see herons, terns, gulls, and, at low tide, a variety of shorebirds. In the winter, Great Cormorants, Brant, Common Eiders, a variety of other waterfowl, gulls, and an occasional raptor may be present.

Snow Shore Landing is another vantage point for the south end of the Nauset marsh system, but it lacks the elevation of Tonset Road. The landing is a good spot to launch a canoe for a trip to New Island or other destinations in the marsh.

New Island, once the southern tip of Coast Guard Beach, is a tiny gem of an island and a superb birding destination during the

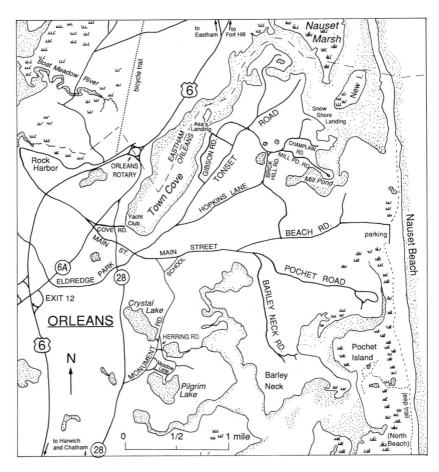

summer and early fall. It is accessible only by boat, but is a fairly easy paddle by canoe from the mainland of Orleans. The best way to visit the island is to go on a tour conducted by the Wellfleet Bay Wildlife Sanctuary. These three-hour trips cover not only the island, but also other destinations in the southern part of the marsh; the excursions are thoroughly enjoyable with great birding. Contact the sanctuary (508-349-2615) for a schedule.

New Island hosts one of the largest tern and Laughing Gull colonies in the northeast. Common Terns are the predominant species, but small numbers of Roseate and Arctic Terns are usually present also. Least Terns usually nest across the channel on the outer beach and are seen routinely. A pair or two of Black Skimmers have nested recently as well. Piping Plovers nest here during most

summers, and from early July through late October, hundreds of shorebirds roost on the island during high tide and can often be observed at close range. Sharp-tailed Sparrows are present in the salt marsh along the western side of the island during the warmer months. In the fall keep an eye out for passing falcons. The tern colony is posted and is strictly off-limits during the nesting season (early May through early August); the aggressive adults are generally quick to let you know when you have wandered too close!

Mill Pond, accessible from the end of Mill Pond Road, has mussel flats that, when exposed at low tide, attract a variety of shorebirds including yellowlegs, dowitchers, plovers, and peep. Occasionally, a Snowy Egret or two will fly in to chase minnows.

Nauset Beach is an excellent spot to look for seabirds from October through April. Over the years, this has been the best location on the Cape to find Harlequin Ducks; some winters, as many as four or five have been present, though in other years, they may be absent altogether. King Eider has also been found here from time to time. The best spot to find these two duck species is a couple of hundred yards north of the parking lot, where a few large rocks are exposed at low tide. Among the more common species that are likely to be present are Common and Red-throated Loons, Horned and Red-necked Grebes, all three species of scoters, Common Eiders, and Red-breasted Mergansers. In the spring and fall, gannets pass by regularly, sometimes by the hundreds, and in winter alcids, most often Razorbills, may appear. Check the beach and small marsh to the north for the occasional Northern Harrier or falcon. A walk through the dunes in the winter may turn up the "Ipswich" form of the Savannah Sparrow, Snow Buntings, or if you're very lucky, a Snowy Owl.

Pochet Island is one of the most beautiful places on the Cape, and it offers fine birding from fall through spring. Access is limited to those with four-wheel-drive vehicles or the energy to hike a mile or so down the beach. This has kept the privately owned island as a virtual sanctuary. A well-kept system of trails covers the island, which has several small swampy areas and one small pond. Most of the island is covered with a dense growth of shrubs, but there are also several groves of pines. During migration a wide variety of migrant passerines and hawks are attracted to this oasis. In the winter, check the pine groves for owls and keep an eye on the sky for hawks. This is one of the most reliable spots around for Rough-legged Hawks and there is always a chance to see something special such as Northern Goshawk, Bald Eagle or Gyrfalcon. The bluff at the south end of the island affords the quiet birder a look at waterfowl feeding in the marsh below, as well as one of the most spectacular vistas imaginable.

Pochet Island is deserted during most of the year. The island's seasonal residents, who generally arrive in late May and stay until October, are very accommodating and welcome most visitors. Please respect their privacy. To reach Pochet, park at the Nauset Beach parking lot and hike south on the beach-buggy trail for a mile or so to the island. Even if there are few birds to be found, a hike to Pochet is well worth the effort.

The end of **Barley Neck Road** offers a view of the back side of Pochet Island and the estuary separating it from the mainland. Watch for hawks over the island and a variety of waterfowl on the water, often including wintering Green-winged Teal and American Wigeon. Eurasian Wigeon has been found here in some years.

Crystal Lake is generally one of the most productive fresh-water ponds in Orleans, but it is rather unpredictable. Hooded Mergansers, Pied-billed Grebes and American Wigeon are often present and Eurasian Wigeon has been found here in the past. The lake can be viewed from a small landing off Monument Road.

Pilgrim Lake is another good duck pond which can be viewed in part from the town beach at the end of Meadow Lane. Look for Pied-billed Grebes, Canvasbacks, Ring-necked Ducks, scaup, and Hooded Mergansers, among others.

EASTHAM

The town of Eastham has some of the top birding spots on the Cape. The topography ranges from the low rolling hills in the southern part of the town to the higher Eastham plains area around Nauset Light. Many acres of prime habitat have been preserved here by the Cape Cod National Seashore.

Fort Hill is one of the premier birding locales in the entire state, and the location affords a magnificent vista over Nauset marsh and bay, Coast Guard Beach, and the distant ocean. The grassy fields, mowed annually by the Cape Cod National Seashore, are among the last remnants of what was once the predominant habitat on Cape Cod. The birding prospects are rich and varied throughout the year, though from late summer through early winter is perhaps the most exciting time.

The fields here are the only known breeding site on the Cape for Bobolinks. During the fall, migrant sparrows are common and carefully searching the thickets will occasionally turn up a Yellow-breasted Chat or some other skulker. This is one of the best areas around for some of the scarcer fall migrants such as Loggerhead Shrike and Western Kingbird. The dense tangles of multiflora rose attract Northern Mockingbirds and other wintering frugivores. When the tide is running abnormally high, over 10½ feet in Boston, during the fall and winter, the marsh floods completely, forcing rails and Sharp-tailed and Seaside Sparrows up into the thickets and dense grass at the base of the hill. The small creek and swampy depression on the southwest corner of the hill also attract migrant and wintering rails, herons, and waterfowl. A few Black-crowned Night-Herons usually spend the winter roosting in the trees here.

Hawks are seen frequently, except in midsummer, and small flights are recorded regularly during migration, particularly in the spring. Among the most common migrants are Northern Harriers, Ospreys, Sharp-shinned Hawks, Broad-winged Hawks (spring only) and American Kestrels. In the winter, harriers, accipiters, falcons, and Rough-legged Hawks may be seen. The extensive marsh attracts high numbers of birds year-round including herons, waterfowl, shorebirds, terns, and gulls. Great Blue Herons are always present; counts in the fall sometimes exceed 100 individuals. During the warmer months, Snowy Egrets, Green-backed Herons, and Black-crowned Night-Herons are generally conspicuous, and a Great Egret, Tricolored Heron, or Yellow-crowned Night-Heron are possible, especially in the late summer. Shorebirds are numerous in May and again from July through November but often are too

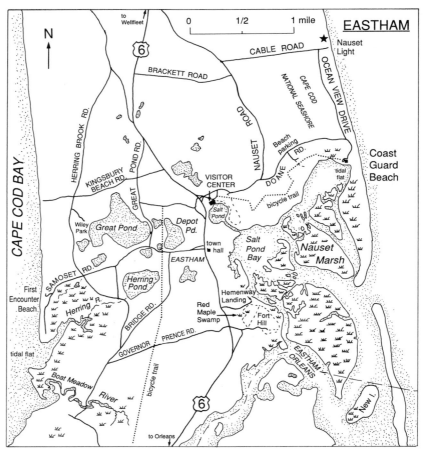

distant to identify easily. A few may roost during high tide in the small tidal pools at the base of the hill.

From late August through September, small flocks of migrant Blue-winged Teal congregate in the marsh. Later in the season flocks of Brant, Canada Geese, Black Ducks, Buffleheads, and Red-breasted Mergansers appear. In midwinter, when the fresh-water ponds freeze over, other species of waterfowl, such as Hooded and Common Mergansers, will visit.

The **Red Maple Swamp**, located off the road that leads to Fort Hill, is a lovely area but usually rather disappointing birdwise. A boardwalk, constructed by the National Seashore, winds through this dark, swampy wood where sphagnum moss and catbrier drape over large twisted maples and tupelos. In the spring and fall, if you're lucky, you may encounter a few migrant passerines.

Hemenway Landing, off Route 6 just to the north of Fort Hill, affords another view of the Nauset marsh system, but the site is best known for its evening flights of night-herons in the summer and fall. At low tide, the exposed flats attract shorebirds and other species, but they tend to be distant and difficult to identify. Herons are present in the marsh during the warmer months and are most conspicuous late in the day when they begin traveling to and from their roosts. The primary roost traditionally has been located to the southwest behind the parking lot. From mid-July through late October, beginning about one and a half to two hours before sunset, Black-crowned Night-Herons start leaving the roost, heading out into the marsh to feed, while Green-backed Herons and Snowy Egrets head into the roost for the night. Counts of night-herons have exceeded 200 birds at times. A few Yellow-crowned Night-Herons are often present as well. Unfortunately, development has recently encroached upon the roost site, and the number of birds using the roost has declined sharply — and so it goes as suburbia rapidly overtakes the Cape.

The **Salt Pond Visitor Center** of the National Seashore is worth a stop for the visiting birder, as a variety of exhibits provide an overview of the natural history of the area. Salt Pond usually has a handful of herons, ducks, and shorebirds in season. Both foot and bicycle trails lead from the visitor center out along the northern edge of Nauset Marsh, ending eventually at Coast Guard Beach. Several spots along the trails offer good views of the marsh and tidal flats. Prairie Warblers are common nesters in the red cedars throughout this area.

Coast Guard Beach is another of the foremost birding locales on the Outer Cape. From the bluff in front of the old Coast Guard station it is possible to scan the ocean for shearwaters (rarely), gannets, sea ducks, terns, kittiwakes, and alcids in season. The tidal flats below the parking lot are packed with shorebirds from July through November as well as a variety of herons, waterfowl, gulls, and terns. The largest concentrations occur a couple of hours before high tide when most of the flats elsewhere in the marsh have become submerged. A walk down the beach during the summer will produce Piping Plovers, several pairs nest here, and Least Terns. At high tide hundreds of shorebirds, primarily peeps and Semi-palmated Plovers, roost on the inside edge of the southern tip. In the fall keep an eye out for passing Peregrine Falcons, Merlins and Northern Harriers. From late fall into the winter, Snow Buntings and Lapland Longspurs may be found in the dunes, and in flight years Snowy Owls are possible.

During the off-season, you can park in the parking lot behind the old Coast Guard station, but in the summer you must park at the lot off Doane Road and take the shuttle bus. Much of the beach is off-limits during the breeding season in order to protect the nesting birds, so heed the posted signs.

Nauset Light is another good vantage for scoping the ocean, offering the possibility for a variety of the typical oceanic species in season.

First Encounter Beach is renowned as a place for land-based observations of pelagic birds during and immediately following storms. Prime conditions typically consist of strong, clearing northwest winds following close on the heels of a coastal northeast storm, as the sea birds that were blown into Cape Cod Bay by the storm stream past the beach in their attempt to find a route back out to the open ocean. However, even ideal conditions do not guarantee a good show; conversely, seemingly unfavorable conditions can occasionally result in some surprising sightings. August through December is the most productive time, but any season offers some possibilities. The rule of thumb is: "if in doubt, check it out!"

The list of potential species at this vantage point reads like a Who's Who of oceanic wanderers, including shearwaters, storm-petrels, gannets, jaegers, kittiwakes, alcids, loons, and all of the sea ducks. Such rarities as Sabine's Gulls, Long-tailed Jaegers, and skuas have been seen here with some regularity. The area has much to offer aside from the possibility of seeing pelagics. Shorebirds, gulls, and terns frequent the tidal flats from May through November. Sharp-tailed Sparrows nest in the marsh, where herons are often present as well. In the fall, falcons regularly pass, and in the late fall to early winter Snow Buntings and Lapland Longspurs can be found.

Great Pond is one of the best freshwater ponds for birding on the Outer Cape. Pied-billed Grebes, Mute Swans, Ring-necked Ducks, scaup, Hooded Mergansers, and Ruddy Ducks are among the more regular species. The pond can be checked from the public parking lot off Great Pond Road and from Wiley Park off Herring Brook Road.

Herring Pond is another pond that can provide good birding in some years. The species to be expected are similar to those on Great Pond. Check it from the town landing off Herring Brook Road.

WELLFLEET

Wellfleet is dominated by the harbor and its associated salt marshes and tidal flats. The uplands are a mix of pitch pine and black oak woods and open bearberry heath. Freshwater kettle ponds cover an extensive area, as do the Herring River Valley and its associated freshwater wetlands and floodplain.

Wellfleet has something to offer the birder year-round. No one place is best at all seasons, however, there are several "must visit" areas.

Massachusetts Audubon Society's Wellfleet Bay Wildlife Sanctuary is the first stop as you enter Wellfleet from the south on Route 6. This 700-acre sanctuary is a microcosm of the Cape in the

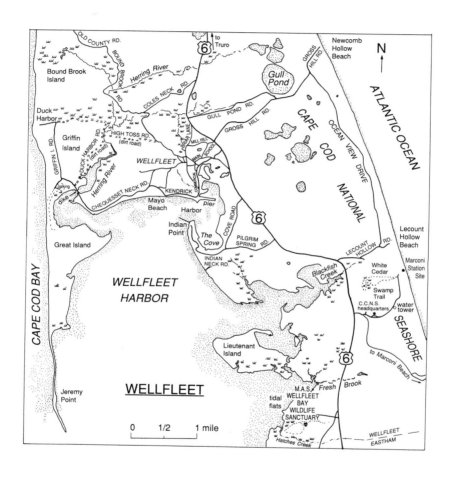

variety of habitats that are found there. The pitch pine/oak woods, open fields, heathlands, freshwater ponds, salt marshes, tidal flats, and beaches offer a wide range of birding opportunities. All seasons can be productive.

In the spring, the best birding is along the Silver Spring Trail, which skirts a freshwater pond created by the damming of Silver Spring Brook. This is one of the best warbler spots on the Cape; as many as 25 species have been seen in one day. In recent years, rare species such as Cerulean, Prothonotary, Kentucky and Hooded Warblers, and Louisiana Waterthrush have been seen here. In addition, a number of other passerines including thrushes, vireos, tanagers, orioles, and sparrows can be found in the trees and thickets surrounding the pond. Wood Ducks and Green-winged and Blue-winged Teal can often be found on the pond, and an Eastern Screech-Owl or two, usually birds rehabilitated at the sanctuary, frequently inhabit the cavities in the area.

Summer and fall, and spring to a lesser degree, are the best times to see shorebirds at the sanctuary. By following the Goose Pond Trail, you will reach Goose Pond, several salt marsh tide pools beyond, and eventually the beach, all excellent areas for shorebirds. Stilt, Solitary, and Pectoral Sandpipers are seen regularly in addition to the more common species. In September look for large concentrations of Greater Yellowlegs, up to 150 or more, and Snowy Egrets, up to 50, in the Goose Pond and in the salt marsh tide pools. Patient perusal of the edges of the Goose Pond may produce a rail during the fall. The best time to bird the tidal flats, which are reached by following the Goose Pond Trail to Try Island and taking the boardwalk across the marsh, is on an incoming tide, one to three hours after low tide. At that time the birds are close to the marsh and beach, rather than spread out over the extensive flats. In the late summer and fall, in addition to the numerous shorebirds, Common, Roseate, Least, Forster's and Black Terns, as well as an occasional Black Skimmer, can be seen resting on the flats. Of special interest are the Whimbrels, which frequent the marsh to feed on fiddler crabs during July and August. During the day, 10 to 20 birds can be seen, but as evening approaches their numbers swell as birds from elsewhere gather before departing for roosting areas to the south; counts as high as 200 have been recorded at this time.

In addition to the trails, the sanctuary has a book/gift shop and numerous natural history programs for adults and children. Included are guided walks, birding tours, boat trips, and field classes.

The **Marconi Station** area of the Cape Cod National Seashore is located just north of the Wellfleet Bay Sanctuary on the east side of Route 6. The road into the site goes through a sparsely vegetated area where Horned Larks and occasionally a pair of Killdeer nest. This is one of the last areas on the Cape where Vesper Sparrows still breed; look for them around the headquarters building and along the road out toward the water tower. During the fall migration, a variety of sparrows can generally be found here, often including rarer species such as Lark, Clay-colored, or Grasshopper Sparrows. The observation deck at the Marconi Station is one of the better hawk watching sites on the Cape, both in spring and fall. The White Cedar Swamp Trail typically has few birds during the day, but at night the intrepid birder may be rewarded with a calling Northern Saw-whet Owl or Eastern Screech-Owl, both of which have nested here. Whip-poor-wills are also present during the summer.

Wellfleet Harbor, accessible from the town pier off Commercial Street, offers fine early winter birding from late October into early January. During this time the birder is likely to see Red-throated and Common Loons, Horned Grebes, Brant, eiders, Oldsquaws, scoters, and, if lucky, a Red-necked Grebe or Harlequin Duck. Alcids also may be seen, particularly after storms; check around the pier for Dovekies, Razorbills, or murres.

Another good spot for checking Wellfleet Harbor is from Indian Point at the end of Indian Neck Road.

The **Dike** on Chequessett Neck Road leading out to Griffin Island is a good spot to check at any season. The Herring River flows under the dike and is often one of the few areas of open water in winter when everything else has frozen. At low tide, in season, shorebirds, herons, and gulls can be seen feeding in the shallow water. At high tide in the spring and fall, ducks, predominantly Black Ducks and Mallards, come into this area to feed, giving the birder a good close look. In recent years, especially in the fall, as many as three or four Ospreys have been seen, just after the tide turns, feeding on menhaden and white perch.

Duck Harbor Road, the dirt road running north along the west side of the river, and **High Toss Road**, which branches off to the right, can be good places to find migrant passerines and hawks. During the winter this is one of the better areas to look for Northern Shrikes. The roads can be very rough and are often closed to vehicle traffic.

Duck Harbor, the beach at the end of Griffin Island Road, is a good winter birding spot, especially at high tide during an easterly wind. Red-necked Grebes, eiders, scoters, goldeneyes, Red-breasted Mergansers, and occasionally, whales and seals can be seen here.

Lecount Hollow Beach and **Newcomb Hollow Beach** both provide good views of the ocean and the possibility of finding gannets, sea ducks, gulls, terns, and, rarely, pelagics.

TRURO

Truro, one of the quietest towns on Cape Cod, is characterized by pitch pine woods and rolling bearberry heath dissected by old outwash valleys such as the Pamet River Valley and Long Nook Valley. Even though it is the most rural of the Cape's towns, there is only a handful of good birding spots.

Pamet Harbor, which has sanded in rather badly in recent years, has deteriorated as a birding spot but is still worth a quick look as a few shorebirds and terns utilize the sandy flats during the warmer months and a few ducks are usually present in the winter.

The end of **Great Hollow Road**, off Route 6, offers an expansive view over Cape Cod Bay and the possibility of seeing many sea ducks, particularly during migration. At times, thousands of Red-breasted Mergansers have amassed here, and gannets can be numerous during spring and fall movements. Pelagics are possible as well, especially after northeasterly storms.

Highland Light is one of the better hawk-watching sites on the Cape. Park in the small parking area and watch for hawks approaching from the south. A good view of the ocean can be had from the end of Coast Guard Road a short distance to the north.

Pond Road at its terminus offers another broad view over Cape Cod Bay with birds similar to those at Great Hollow Road.

Head of the Meadow Beach provides a good view of the ocean and potential sightings of gannets, sea ducks, and occasionally pelagics in season. The bicycle trail at the north end of the parking lot runs north between the marsh and pine barrens, ending at Pilgrim Lake. It can be well worth exploring, particularly during migration, for land birds, hawks and marsh birds, and affords a lovely walk at any season.

The **Pilgrim Heights area** is a premier spring hawk-watching site. The Cape narrows to its thinnest point here, funneling the raptors into easy viewing range; there is always the chance of

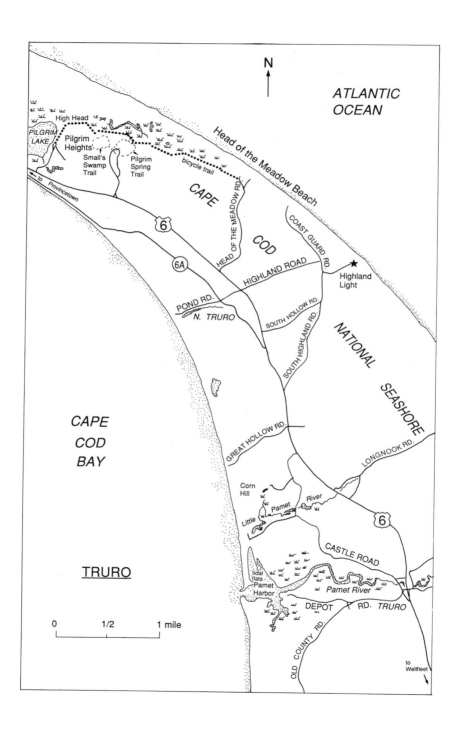

encountering a warbler wave as well. Maps of the area are available at the trail head and at the Cape Cod National Seashore visitor centers in Eastham, South Wellfleet, and Provincetown.

Hawk watching here is best from the overlooks on the Small's Swamp Trail. If you bear right at the first fork in the trail, you will come to the first of two overlooks; continue down the trail and you will arrive at the second. Either overlook is good for viewing, though most birders prefer the second. The hawks appear out over the dunes, frequently right below the lookout, or they approach from over the woods to the southeast. The hawks are often seen going north, "outbound," as well as south on their return after reaching land's end in Provincetown. The most commonly seen species are the Sharp-shinned Hawk, Broad-winged Hawk, and American Kestrel, with smaller numbers of Ospreys, Turkey Vultures, Red-tailed Hawks, Merlins, and Northern Harriers. A Peregrine Falcon or Bald Eagle will occasionally spice up the day. Northern Harriers nest in the dunes nearby, and in the early spring the males can be seen performing their remarkable courtship flights. Unlike hawk watching at inland sites, the birds at Pilgrim Heights are not just dots in the sky but can be seen at fairly close range, sometimes amazingly close; photographers bring your camera.

The bicycle trail that winds along the edge of the marsh can be a good place to look for warblers and other passerines. Follow the Pilgrim Spring Trail until you come to the paved bicycle trail, which you can take in either direction, left to High Head or right to Head of the Meadow. Be mindful of bikers; they have the right of way. On a good migration day, the thickets of shadbush, blueberry, and winterberry along the edges of the trail can be alive with small birds.

Pilgrim Lake is gradually sanding in and rarely has much to offer. You can easily and quickly check it however, by carefully pulling off Route 6 onto the sandy shoulder. During the winter, the flocks of roosting gulls will sometimes include an Iceland Gull or a Glaucous Gull. Ducks, aside from the ubiquitous Black Duck, are few and far between, although Common Mergansers are seen with some regularity in the winter.

PROVINCETOWN

On a day-to-day basis, no other town on Cape Cod offers the birding potential of Provincetown, and the visiting birder would do well to allow at least a day for exploring this fascinating community. Composed entirely of sand washed northward from Cape Cod's eroding

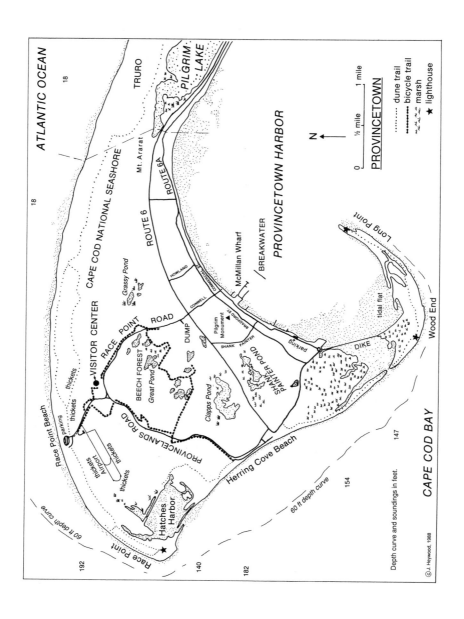

eastern shore and virtually surrounded by water, the area, with its human and natural history, has been deeply sculpted by the sea. Almost every aspect of the area, its bird life, plant life, geology, and human culture, is remarkably unique and reflects the ocean's pervasive influence.

Appropriately for a community with such a strong marine heritage, there is probably no place in eastern North America that offers quite the potential for seeing pelagic birds. Although a few seabirds are generally present at any season, during the fall and early winter the concentrations can be spectacular.

In the spring, migrating songbirds and hawks are funneled northward along the Outer Cape and, reluctant to cross the water, become concentrated in Provincetown, often in large numbers. In the fall, the area provides the first landfall for migrants that have drifted off course over the Gulf of Maine. Only during the mid-summer, when the avian population is low and the human population high, does the birding slow down, though even then the visiting birder will generally find something of interest.

The **Provincetown Dump**, off Race Point Road, is often frequented by vultures or eagles that may be in the area, and during the late fall and winter keep an eye out for Iceland or Glaucous Gulls, and possibly a Lesser Black-backed Gull.

The **Beech Forest** is without a doubt the finest spot on Cape Cod to witness the spring passerine migration and is also worth birding in the fall, particularly from late August through September when warblers are passing south. It is an oasis among the dunes, with small marshy ponds surrounded by beeches, alders, six species of pines and—most notably—oaks. Where oaks predominate is where you are most likely to encounter spring migrants, though fall migrants are more widespread and apt to be anywhere. Species to be expected include all of the typical eastern Massachusetts migrants. The following descriptions pertain primarily to the spring season when the location of the birds is more predictably associated with specific habitats. Some of the better spots in the Beech Forest are the following.

Wooden Bridge   This area adjacent to the parking lot is among the most consistently productive. If any birds are around at all, there is apt to be a pocket of them here. Check the oaks on the opposite side of Race Point Road as well.

Far end of "Wood Duck" Pond   The trail in this section, with its large oaks and beeches, is the most consistently productive, particularly early in the morning. It is sheltered from most of the raw ocean breezes and catches the warmth of the rising sun. Several

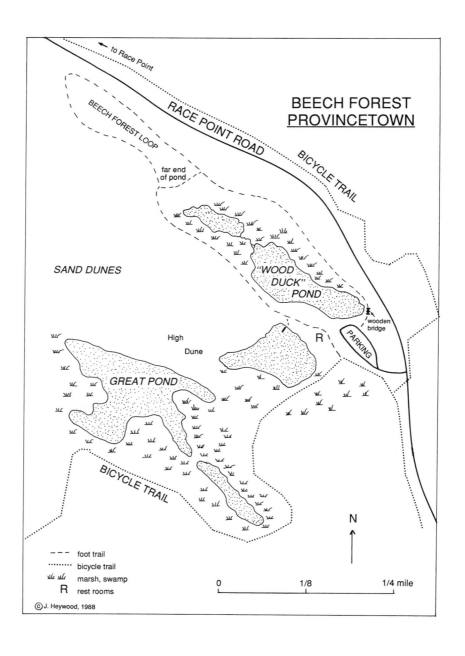

BEECH FOREST
PROVINCETOWN

to Race Point

RACE POINT ROAD

BEECH FOREST LOOP

BICYCLE TRAIL

far end
of pond

SAND DUNES

"WOOD
DUCK"
POND

wooden
bridge

High

Dune

R

PARKING

GREAT POND

BICYCLE TRAIL

N

– – –   foot trail
....   bicycle trail
ᵛ⟋ᵛ⟋   marsh, swamp
R   rest rooms

0   1/8   1/4 mile

ⓒ J. Heywood, 1988

"layers" of birding potential are present here, from the moist, swampy hollow below to the neck-stiffening tops of the highest trees on the hillside above. On a good day it can be difficult to decide whether to look up, down, or straight ahead!

Other spots in the Beech Forest that are worth checking for migrants are the bicycle trail on the northeast side of Race Point Road; the oaks at the northwest corner of the forest; the main trail from the split rail fence to the rest rooms; and the bicycle trail from the rest rooms south between the ponds.

During weekend afternoons the parking lot and main trail become cluttered with weekenders who are often noisy (portable stereos at full volume are not uncommon) and who can hamper birding efforts; try to arrive early to beat the rush. Access to the parking lot is off Race Point Road.

The **Cape Cod National Seashore Visitor Center** sits on a high bluff overlooking most of the northern portions of town and is another good place to watch hawks, however, the light is often poor here. Watch from the parking lot, or better still, go to the observation deck at the top of the building from which the outer dunes can be watched for falcons and accipiters.

The **Provincetown Airport and vicinity** is mainly of interest in the fall when the many thickets attract numerous passerines, and accipiters and falcons frequently pass over. Park at the Race Point Beach parking lot and walk back to the airport (the airport parking lot is reserved for customers). From here you can proceed southwest following the line of wet thickets that extend from the parking lot to the end of the runway; keep well away from the runway. If you are ambitious and continue far enough—about one and a quarter miles—you will end up at Hatches Harbor. On a good day the complete route, although arduous, is well worth the effort. An alternative is to walk down the outer beach from the Race Point parking lot and walk back along the airport; this loop combines the possibilities of seeing both seabirds and land birds. Another walk that can be productive for finding passerines begins across the road from the airport and follows the densely vegetated ravines that run eastward through the dunes for about two to three miles. With the passage of a cold front in the fall, this entire area can be hopping with migrants, offering some lively birding. During the late fall and winter, Northern Harriers and an occasional Rough-legged Hawk or Northern Shrike, in flight years, can often be found here.

The **Race Point parking lot** is one of the finest locations in eastern North America to watch for seabirds, with the potential for a diverse and exciting array of pelagics, particularly from late August through February. All of the regular northwest Atlantic pelagics have been seen here, and the more common species are seen with some regularity and occasionally in large numbers when conditions are favorable.

Exactly why these birds occur with such consistency in this vicinity remains uncertain, though a variety of factors are likely to be involved. Undoubtedly, Provincetown's location, thrusting prominently toward the Gulf of Maine, results in many seabirds being intercepted by this land mass as they move southward during the fall. The rich Stellwagen Bank, host to an abundance of marine birds and mammals, lies just a few miles to the north and certainly contributes to many of the sightings from land. Another important factor appears to be the presence of over 100-feet-deep water close to shore in this area. Presumably this sharp drop-off results in some upwelling and, in conjunction with the strong rips and currents characteristic of the region, provides a source of plentiful food. This deep water line can be seen from the parking lot, if the sea is fairly calm, some 800 yards out from shore where the shallow, light blue water turns to a deep, dark blue. Farther to the west this line occurs progessively closer to shore and is closest, roughly 200 yards away, just north of the tip of Race Point itself.

Generally the best weather conditions for producing birds at Race Point consist of cloudy skies with light to moderate winds, although during the peak season, late August to November, a few birds can usually be found under most any conditions. When the winds are strong, over 40 miles per hour, from the northeast, viewing is very difficult particularly if it is raining. The dunes in front of the parking lot have built up to the point that it is nearly impossible to see the water from the comfort of a car, making it necessary to brave the elements. Both the bath house and the old Coast Guard station can afford some protection from the worst of the weather. Viewing pelagics from land is rarely a comfortable endeavor at any location.

Strong northwest winds following a northeast storm can provide a good show as the pelagics that were blown into Cape Cod Bay by the storm stream back out into the open ocean. During the warmer months fog can result in a few pelagics drifting in close to land, but you must be on hand at the precise moment that the fog clears because little if anything can be seen before, and the birds move out rapidly as visibility improves. Be forewarned, however, that the ocean here can be as barren as anywhere; finding pelagics is always a hit or miss proposition.

There is probably no finer place in the Northeast to see jaegers from land; on many days from mid-August through October, with a little patience and a sharp eye, you can often see at least one or two jaegers and at times counts of 20 or more are possible. The Parasitic Jaeger is by far the most common species, but Pomarine Jaegers are seen from time to time and the Long-tailed Jaeger is reported very rarely. You may also see impressive numbers of shearwaters; counts in the hundreds and even thousands are not uncommon in some years, especially after storms. The Greater Shearwater is the predominant species, but the Sooty Shearwater is also possible, particularly in the early summer, and during the summer and early fall of some years, Cory's can be found. This is an excellent spot as well to look for Manx Shearwaters from August through October. While looking for birds, keep an eye out for spouting whales, which are present throughout the year with the largest numbers generally occurring during the spring and fall. Fin and humpback whales typically are the most common, but minke and right whales are possible and white-sided dolphins are seen rarely. "Have you seen any whales?" is a question often hurled at the scope-wielding birder.

Race Point, when conditions are favorable, is unsurpassed for close observations of pelagics from land. Deep water is less than 200 yards offshore here and shearwaters, alcids, and others can often be seen feeding at remarkably close range. Much of the information on the Race Point parking lot pertains to this area as well. During the winter months, murres, Razorbills, and guillemots have been found regularly along the outer beach between the point and the parking lot. A calm sea at this time of year is best as then the alcids can often be seen sitting and feeding along the deep-water line. Access is by foot or, during certain seasons only, four-wheel-drive vehicle— check at the seashore ranger station on Race Point Road for regulations.

Hatches Harbor, as its name indicates, once served as a harbor but has now sanded-in, a fate to which every body of water in Provincetown seems destined. This "harbor" now consists of a small patch of salt marsh and some tidal flats, separated from the bay by a spit of sand. On the east it is bordered by the remains of a dike; to the east of the dike lies the airport with its border of wet thickets. The flats and spit attract large numbers of gulls year-round and terns from July to October, and occasionally the rarer members of their clan can be found. Lesser Black-backed Gulls have been found here with some regularity in the fall. A few shorebirds are also usually present in season. Harbor seals frequently haul out on the spit during the winter. Although the habitat is limited here, the "land's-end" location makes it the type of spot where almost anything is apt to drop in. Access is by foot or four-wheel-drive vehicle.

Herring Cove is another vantage point for viewing seabirds but, because the observer is at a low elevation, and the birds are usually at a considerable distance from shore, it is generally less productive than the Race Point area, which is visible to the north. Poor light can also be a problem during the afternoon. Large numbers of terns feed here from late summer to early fall and often attract jaegers into easy viewing range. Various sea ducks are common during the colder months.

Shank Painter Pond is one of those places that looks like it should be full of birds yet rarely produces anything. Wood Ducks are sometimes present and night-herons occasionally fish the edges, but otherwise there is little to be said about the area. It is easy to check from Route 6, however, and should not be passed by without a quick look.

Vesper Sparrows may nest in the dunes in this part of town, as well as around the airport, and watch the grassy edges of the highway for sparrows during migration. The thickets, like elsewhere in town, may harbor migrants.

Wood End, Long Point, and dike, located at the west end of Provincetown Harbor, make up a typical barrier beach with salt marsh and mud flats on the inside and scrubby thickets in the dune hollows. Black-crowned Night-herons have nested here as have a few Common and Least Terns. The tidal flats attract a small number of shorebirds in season and the thickets may have a few migrant land birds in the fall. During the late summer, large flocks of terns roost on the flats at low tide and generally include good numbers of Roseate Terns. Summering Black-legged Kittiwakes, invariably immatures, have appeared here regularly in June and July, as have immature Arctic Terns. A few pelagics are sometimes seen off the beach in summer and fall.

You can park at the west-end rotary (in summer get there early) and walk out the dike to Wood End. This should be done cautiously and only at low tide, which is when the birding is best. Be very aware of the tide as the higher tides can cover the dike.

Provincetown Harbor is one of the best known and most frequently birded locations in Provincetown. It is primarily of interest in winter when it attracts cormorants, a variety of sea ducks, white-winged gulls, kittiwakes, and alcids, particularly after storms. You can check the harbor from several vantage points, all accessible from Commercial Street. The best of these is McMillan Wharf, which extends well out into the harbor and offers the opportunity for excellent views of many of the birds. Alcids, when they are present (infrequently), are often very close to the wharf, even underneath it, so be sure to look over the edge. Photographers will find this an exceptional place to photograph several species of birds that normally can be approached only from a boat. During the winter you can drive to the end of the wharf, but pay attention to the "No Parking" signs.

A couple of other public parking lots located off Commercial Street provide good views of the harbor. The best is toward the west end adjacent to the Center for Coastal Studies. From there, guillemots have been seen near the center of the harbor in some years. Extensive mud flats are located along the east end of the harbor at low tide, but they are rather unproductive.

Although some of the more productive birding spots in Provincetown are outlined above, keep in mind that the dunes throughout town are full of wet, swampy thickets and during a good wave any of them are apt to have birds. Keep an eye out for pockets of birds as you drive around the area and be prepared to do a little exploring of your own. Be aware, however, that parking is prohibited along Race Point Road, Provincelands Road, and sections of Route 6. This ban is strictly enforced and with good reason as the sand is very soft in many areas; stick to the designated parking areas.

Because parking is rather limited, and many areas are not accessible by paved road, considerable walking is necessary to cover the region well, particularly when looking for land birds. Another means of transportation you may wish to consider is a bicycle. There is an excellent, though rather rigorous, bicycle trail that covers much of the town, and many of the areas outlined in this chapter are readily accessible by bike. Those with a four-wheel-drive vehicle can obtain a permit to drive on the beach out to Race Point at the Cape Cod National Seashore headquarters on Race Point Road. Access to the dune trails by vehicle is tightly controlled and becoming increasingly restricted, so be sure to obtain the proper permits before venturing onto any of them.

4 MONOMOY

Located within the town of Chatham at the elbow of Cape Cod, Monomoy is the most northeasterly of a series of islands that fringe New England's southern shore. Unlike the other islands, which are glacial formations resulting from the Pleistocene ice sheet, Monomoy, composed of sand washed southward from Cape Cod's eroding eastern shore, is entirely a creation of the sea. As such, Monomoy is a classic barrier island, with surf-battered dunes on its eastern shore that gradually flatten out to salt marsh and mud flats on its western shore. The ocean is continually reshaping Monomoy's approximately 2500 acres, and at various times in its history, it has been a peninsula, an island, or a series of islands.

For the first half of this century, Monomoy was a peninsula connected to the Chatham mainland at Morris Island and was accessible by beach buggy, which made it a popular birdwatching area, much visited by the famed Ludlow Griscom and other birders of his time. In 1958 an April storm "islandized" the peninsula by breaching the beach just below Morris Island, creating the cut-through that still exists today. Local rumor has it that this April storm was aided and abetted by a few shovel-wielding local fishermen eager for a quicker route from Nantucket Sound to the ocean!

Twenty years later, in February 1978, a severe northeaster combined with extremely high tides "bi-islandized" Monomoy, creating a second cut-through just north of Inward Point, about one and a half miles south of the first cut. Consequently, Monomoy now consists of two islands: a shrinking, unstable north island approximately two miles long and a more stable and enlarging south island about six miles long.

For most of the eighteenth and nineteenth centuries, Monomoy was inhabited by the citizens of a small but active fishing village—Whitewash Village—located along the perimeter of what is now called the Powder Hole, then a rather sizable harbor. During the last part of the nineteenth century, the harbor began to sand in, and by the turn of the century, few year-round inhabitants remained. In 1944 Monomoy became a National Wildlife Refuge, and in 1970 the island was afforded even more extensive protection as a result of its designation as a National Wilderness Area. Since the U. S. Fish & Wildlife Service gained control of the island, employees have slowly but steadily been dismantling the old buildings, so that only the old lighthouse and a couple of run-down shacks remain standing.

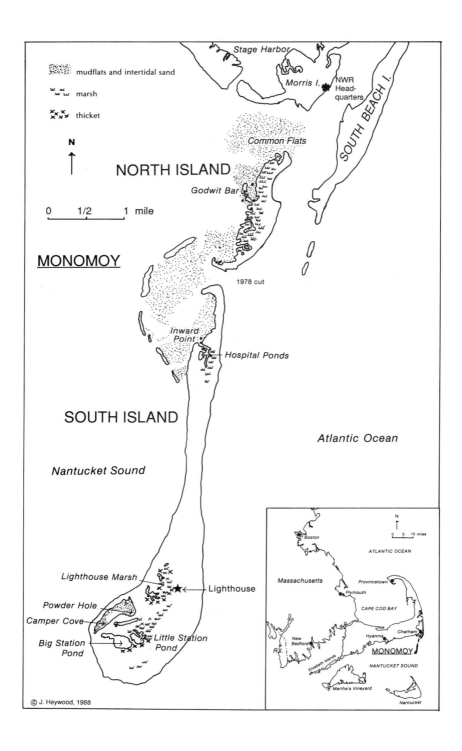

mudflats and intertidal sand

marsh

thicket

N

NORTH ISLAND

Common Flats

Godwit Bar

0   1/2   1 mile

MONOMOY

1978 cut

Inward Point

Hospital Ponds

SOUTH ISLAND

Atlantic Ocean

Nantucket Sound

Stage Harbor

Morris I.

NWR Headquarters

SOUTH BEACH I.

Lighthouse Marsh

Lighthouse

Powder Hole

Camper Cove

Big Station Pond

Little Station Pond

© J. Heywood, 1988

N

0   5   10 miles

ATLANTIC OCEAN

Massachusetts

Provincetown

Plymouth

CAPE COD BAY

Boston

Hyannis

Chatham

New Bedford

R.I.

MONOMOY

Elizabeth Islands

NANTUCKET SOUND

Martha's Vineyard

Nantucket

Monomoy's ornithological history began during the era of the sportsmen/naturalists in the late 1800s. The hordes of migrating waterfowl and shorebirds attracted many of these gentlemen gunners, resulting in the formation of the Monomoy Brant Club in 1862. Though most of these men were primarily interested in hunting, there were some fine naturalists among them, and their records provide us with considerable information on at least a portion of the bird life at that time.

Much more complete information on the island's bird life resulted from Ludlow Griscom's interest in the area. Griscom was the first to exploit Monomoy's potential as one of the most exciting birding locations on the East Coast and during his lifetime he made over 300 trips down what was then a peninsula. Ironically, Monomoy became separated from the mainland just a few months before Griscom's death in 1959.

During the 1960s the ornithological coverage of Monomoy reached its apex. In 1960 the Massachusetts Audubon Society, under a cooperative agreement with the U. S. Fish & Wildlife Service, began conducting beachbuggy tours of the island to view wildlife. Led by a series of young guides with an insatiable passion for birds, these tours quickly became very popular and ran almost daily during the peak summer season. During the late 1960s a banding operation under the direction of Massachusetts Audubon's James Baird was conducted on the south end, based in the old lighthouse that had been purchased by the Society in 1964. Consequently, for a few years Monomoy received a level of coverage that is not likely to be matched again. The designation of Monomoy as a National Wilderness Area eliminated vehicle access

B. VAN DUSEN

and, combined with changes in the physical structure of the island and surrounding waters, made the tours increasingly difficult to operate, and they were terminated after the 1975 season. However, both Massachusetts Audubon and the Cape Cod Museum of Natural History now offer walking tours of the island. Staff naturalists offer trips to both the north and south islands (see *Access* page 96). A more detailed history of Monomoy is available in *Monomoy Wilderness*, a delightful booklet published by the Massachusetts Audubon Society in 1972, which is, unfortunately, out of print.

Birding on Monomoy varies considerably on the two islands. Bird life on the north island is most interesting from May through October when large numbers of shorebirds and terns are present, whereas birding on the south island is best from August through November when migrant land birds, raptors, waterfowl, and some of the rarer shorebirds can be found.

The *north island* consists entirely of dunes, salt marsh, and mud flats and attracts hordes of migrating and nesting terns, gulls, and shorebirds. The largest concentrations of birds are generally found shortly before or soon after high tide as they feed along the edge of the flats and marsh in a quarter-mile stretch extending from the extreme north end, south to Godwit Bar. However, during the time of most high tides this area is flooded, and the birds are often forced farther down the island or over to South Beach Island to the east.

Until recently one of the largest Common Tern colonies in the Northeast, with over 3,000 pairs, was located in the dunes on the extreme north end of the island. The terns have been plagued with a variety of problems, however, and the colony now consists of only a few hundred terns dispersed in small groups on marsh hummocks throughout the island. Roseate Terns have become erratic nesters, but some can be found roosting on the flats during the spring and early summer, and large numbers of postbreeders from other colonies are present from late July through mid-September. One or two pairs of Arctic Terns still attempt to nest each year, and a few migrants can occasionally be found in May. In some years recently, up to several hundred immature Arctic Terns have been present during June and July. Least Terns nest sporadically, sometimes in considerable numbers, but their presence is completely unpredictable from year to year and even from week to week. An additional six species of terns occur more or less regularly, and Black Skimmers have nested on rare occasions (as many as three pairs in 1986) and are often seen in the late summer.

A colony of several hundred pairs of Laughing Gulls, one of only two in the state, was located on the north end of the island, but like the terns its population has declined recently, and only a few pairs remain. In 1984 a pair of Common Black-headed Gulls nested among the Laughing Gulls, establishing a first breeding record for the United States. Nesting Great Black-backed and Herring Gulls have occupied the remainder of the north island as well as most of the south island; a 1984 census of both islands yielded approximately 20,000 pairs, giving the islands the distinction of having one of the largest gull colonies in North America. Keep in mind that the tern and Laughing Gull nesting areas are strictly off-limits.

Nesting shorebirds are represented by a pair or two of Piping Plovers and a burgeoning population of American Oystercatchers and Willets. After an absence of a century or more, the latter two species both re-established themselves as nesters in the early 1970s and are currently thriving with over 10 pairs of oyster-catchers and more than 30 pairs of Willets occupying the north island. Spotted Sandpipers, once common, are now rare as nes-ters. Certainly the most spectacular avian event in the area is the shorebird migration, which peaks in late May and again in late July to early August, when several thousand birds may be present. Even more impressive than the numbers is the variety, which is greatest from late August to mid-September. An incredible 46 species of shorebirds, from every corner of the globe, have been recorded on Monomoy. Among the regularly occurring species, the very local Hudsonian Godwit is a feature, and in recent years counts during the early August peak have averaged between 100 and 150 individ-uals. Buff-breasted and Baird's Sandpipers can also be found on occasion, though they are more frequent on the south island.

Herons are commonly seen in the marsh, and although Snowy Egrets and Black-crowned Night-Herons predominate, all of the regularly occurring northeastern herons are seen from time to time. Although the water birds are the main attraction on the north island, a few other species are worth looking for. Sharp-tailed Sparrows are common nesters throughout the marsh, and in some years Seaside Sparrows have been found along the tidal creeks. Horned Larks and Savannah Sparrows are common nesters in the dunes, where the observer might also flush a Short-eared Owl in any season. During migration you should constantly be on the lookout for passing Peregrine Falcons, Merlins, Northern Harriers, and Sharp-shinned Hawks, and occasionally a few land bird migrants can be flushed from the grass. Lapland Longspurs and Snow Buntings are commonly seen in the late fall and winter.

Most of *South Monomoy* is comprised of scantily vegetated dunes, and the bird life, with the exception of nesting gulls, Horned

Larks, and Savannah Sparrows, is sparse indeed. Toward South Monomoy's northern terminus just inside Inward Point, there is a small area of salt marsh, the so-called Hospital Ponds which are now largely sanded over. Two to three pairs of oystercatchers nest along the beach here. Formerly one of the finest land bird thickets on the island, Wildcat Swamp was located on what is now the northeast corner of the south island; but this wet swale, which provided the only cover for a couple of miles in any direction, has been claimed by the sea, leaving only a few dead shrubs and pines. From Inward Point southward for a mile or so there is a small, sprawling colony of Black-crowned Night-Herons and Snowy Egrets.

In contrast, the south end of South Monomoy has freshwater ponds and marshes, and dense, wet thickets of bayberry, beach plum, and poison ivy (everywhere!), providing the primary attraction for both birds and birders. When conditions are right during fall migration and more rarely in the spring, this area offers some of the most exciting and challenging birding on the East Coast. The hub of avian activity here is the Station Ponds, which lie to the southwest of the lighthouse: Big Station Pond to the west and the smaller, more marshy, Little Station Pond to the east. Quantities of herons, ducks, and shorebirds frequent these ponds, and the numerous, dense thickets ringing their perimeters attract numbers of migrant passerines on good days.

Just to the west of the lighthouse is the Lighthouse Marsh, actually a group of very small shallow ponds and wet depressions interspersed among more dense thickets and a few scrub pines, which represent some of the few trees on the island. These ponds are also good places to see ducks and herons and the thickets for migrant land birds. To the north of the lighthouse are extensive Hudsonia moors that can be worth checking in the early fall for Buff-breasted and Baird's Sandpipers, Lesser Golden-Plovers, and Whimbrels.

On the southwestern corner of the island lies the Powder Hole and the adjacent Camper Cove, an excellent area for shorebirds, terns, and gulls. This cove was tidal, but sand washing around the point is about to close off the flow of water from Nantucket Sound, the same process that formed the Station Ponds. South and southwest of Big Station Pond are a series of thickets, many of which border small, damp, grassy "sedgeflats."

On a good day on the south island, most of the typical northeastern fall migrants can be found, and a list of over 100 species is quite possible. However, a few species that are regular or even common on nearby Morris Island are scarce or absent on Mono-moy. This group of species consists primarily of those that are very reluctant to cross water or that are rather sedentary. Black-capped Chickadees, Blue Jays, Cardinals, House Finches, White-breasted Nuthatches, Hairy Woodpeckers, House Sparrows, and the buteos are all rare at best, and the Tufted Titmouse has yet to be recorded.

It is, of course, the rare and unexpected—the vagrants—that excite most birders, and South Monomoy has a vagrant track record that is unsurpassed, despite the area's coverage. Some of the more typical fall vagrants include Red-headed Woodpecker, Western Kingbird, Yellow-headed Blackbird, Blue Grosbeak, Lark Sparrow, and Clay-colored Sparrow.

When you are looking for coastal migrants, the weather is critical to any observer's success, and nowhere is this more evident than on the south island. When the weather is favorable, which in the fall usually consists of a northwest wind following the passage of a cold front, the birding can be fantastic. However, unlike many other coastal traps, there is a distinct lack of desirable land bird habitat here, resulting in a quick exodus of most of the individuals that may be present immediately after the passage of a cold front. Fortunately, the water bird habitats are more consistently produc-tive, and some good birding is likely on even the slowest of days.

If you are fortunate enough to get to the south end during good weather, you'll have no problem occupying an entire day. Check all of the thickets slowly, including those around the Station Ponds, to the east of Little Station Pond, around the Lighthouse Marsh, between the Powder Hole and Big Station Pond, and espe-cially those on the extreme southwest corner of the island. It seems that many southbound birds tend to build up in these last thickets before leaving the island headed in a southwesterly or westerly direction, and there is a constant turnover here. Always keep an eye on the sky, as Peregrine Falcons, Merlins, Sharp-shinned Hawks, and Northern Harriers pass through regularly in the fall, as do many other diurnal migrants. Short-eared Owls nest in the dunes and might be flushed almost anywhere during any season.

The west end of Big Station Pond and the south and east sides of Little Station Pond are the best spots for shorebirds during dry years. In wet years the series of damp "sedgeflats" south of the Station Ponds are the best bet for shorebirds. Buff-breasted and Baird's Sandpipers can often be found here in early fall as well as Wilson's Phalaropes, Stilt and Pectoral Sandpipers, and Long-billed Dowitchers. Pelagics can sometimes be seen off the south point.

Although the birds are the primary attraction on Monomoy, the visitor who sees only birds has experienced but a portion of this unique and fascinating natural community. Several species of mammals are present on the islands year-round. Whitetail deer are common and generally conspicuous on the south island and seem to thrive despite a severe shortage of winter browse. From November to May, harbor seals are present in large numbers with counts of over 1,000 in recent years, and they are often joined by several individuals of the much rarer gray seal. Muskrats are common around the ponds on the south island and have also been present in some years on North Monomoy, where the only source of fresh water is below ground. Butterflies are conspicuous in the late summer and early fall, and it is possible to see several species in a day. For the botanist, over 160 species of plants have been identified, most around the freshwater habitats on the south island.

Access: When planning a visit, contact the Monomoy National Wildlife Refuge headquarters to obtain the current information about permission and restrictions and boating and weather information. The address is Monomoy National Wildlife Refuge, Morris Island, Chatham, MA 02633 (telephone: 508-945-0594). (In winter, contact Great Meadows National Wildlife Refuge, Weir Hill Road, Sudbury, MA 01776; telephone: 508-443-4661.)

Monomoy can be reached only by boat and is not always an easy place to visit. For those not fortunate enough to have a friend with a boat, the easiest way to reach the islands is either on a guided tour or with one of the private ferry services operating from the Chatham mainland. Those visiting for the first time would do well to take one of the frequent guided tours conducted by the Massachusetts Audubon Society, organized by its Wellfleet Bay Wildlife Sanctuary, or by the Cape Cod Museum of Natural History. These tours, led by experienced naturalists, are offered both to North Monomoy and to South Monomoy regularly from April through November and infrequently during the winter. Call or write the Society's Wellfleet Bay Wildlife Sanctuary, P.O. Box 236, South Wellfleet, MA 02663 (508-349-2615), or the Cape Cod Museum of Natural History, P. O. Drawer R, Brewster, MA 02631 (508-896-3867) for their current schedules and rates. For those preferring to explore the islands on their own, one or more private ferry services are generally available, but they tend to be rather ephemeral. Contact the refuge headquarters for up-to-date information on these services.

An increasingly popular means of reaching North Monomoy is to canoe or kayak from the beach below the Monomoy refuge parking lot on Morris Island. It's a short and reasonably safe paddle to the island, though the current can be strong, but the trip should be attempted only by experienced canoeists and only when the weather is favorable, i.e., little or no wind and little possibility of fog. When beaching your canoe on the island, be certain it is well above the high-tide line. A floatable, waterproof container for your optics is also advisable.

Anyone attempting to take a craft to Monomoy should be an experienced boater, familiar with the local waters and constantly alert for changes in weather conditions. The weather in the area is very unpredictable and can change suddenly and dramatically. Fog is especially prevalent during the warmer months and can develop literally in a matter of minutes. Do not attempt to take a small boat around the south point as there are treacherous rips there under certain conditions.

Ideally, visits to the north island should be scheduled to coincide with high tide when the shorebirds and terns are concentrated. The tide has little effect on the bird life of the south island. Whichever island you visit, you should keep in mind that no rest room facilities are available and, on the north island, practically no cover except low scrub or dunes, so attend to personal needs before embarking. Bring water or fruit to relieve thirst and a snack and some sort of protection from the sun because there is no shade. A lightweight poncho will provide protection from salt spray during the boat trip for both your optics and yourself. Be prepared to wade to and from the boat. Old sneakers are generally the recommended footwear during the warmer months, but to insure safe footing on the slippery mud flats, you may want something with a sole that can grip securely. The temperature is generally several degrees cooler on Monomoy than on the mainland, and there is no shelter from wind or blowing sand on either island, so dress accordingly. On the south island, poison ivy is virtually everywhere, growing in loose prostrate carpets throughout the dunes and in five- to six-foot-high bushes in the thickets. It is impossible to bird in the area effectively without some contact with the sinister weed. It is a good idea to bring along your favorite ointment if you are allergic to poison ivy; rubbing alcohol will diminish the effects if it is applied to exposed skin shortly after contact with the plant. (Old hands often swear by washing exposed portions of the skin with salt water before leaving the island.) On occasion, ticks and mosquitos can be a nuisance on the south island also. On the north island, the only insect problem occurs during July and August when green-headed flies are on the prowl. Insect repellants will help, and long pants are recommended for protection against all these forces.

When visiting Monomoy, particularly the north island, during the breeding season (May to early August), keep in mind that birds are nesting everywhere on the island. Some of the primary nesting areas are posted and off-limits, but no matter where you are, except on portions of the outer beach, you are probably keeping birds off their nests. The best strategy to minimize disturbance is to keep moving and not linger too long in any one place. Certain portions of the refuge are closed during the nesting season, and visitors should always contact the headquarters ahead of time for current regulations (508-945-0594).

5 PELAGIC BIRDING

With the proliferation of whale watching boats, the visiting birder has ample opportunity to head seaward to observe pelagic birds. Though trips aboard tour boats, ferries, and fishing party boats are available, none goes very far offshore or can compare to the whale watching tours that are offered from mid-April to the end of October. Provincetown is the port of departure for the majority of these trips, but occasionally trips leave from Dennis and Barnstable. Most of these trips last four to five hours.

Although Cape Cod Bay can offer good sea birding during the spring and fall, in summer the pelagics are usually further offshore. Stellwagen Bank north of Provincetown usually hosts the largest number and greatest variety of birds and is the most desirable destination for birders. Check with the whale watching boats (listed in the local yellow pages of the phone book) to find out where the whales are and whether they are feeding. Feeding concentrations of whales frequently attract large numbers of birds, but if the whales aren't feeding, the seabirds may be widely scattered.

The number and species of pelagic birds in Cape Cod waters are highly variable from month to month (and even from week to week at times), but some general trends hold true.

April can be an interesting month with a diversity of sightings, but the weather is often stormy offshore and the whale watching boats typically remain in Cape Cod Bay looking for right whales, which are a particular specialty in early spring. Though pelagic species are generally scarce inshore during this season, Black Guillemots are often seen inside of Long Point, Provincetown, and sea ducks such as Black, White-winged, and Surf Scoters, Common Eiders, and Oldsquaws feed just offshore of Long Point. Sightings of Red-throated and Common Loons, various other sea ducks, and Razorbills are also possible. Though gannets can be found in the bay in spring, they are more numerous offshore where Northern Fulmars, Red Phalaropes, Black-legged Kittiwakes, and a few alcids are often present as well.

May is a transitional month. A few of the wintering Iceland and Glaucous Gulls and alcids may linger until midmonth, while migrants heading to more northerly breeding sites, such as Leach's Storm-Petrels, Red-necked Phalaropes, and jaegers pass through in small numbers. Parasitic Jaegers can sometimes be seen inshore off Herring Cove and Race Point in Provincetown, especially where terns and small gulls are feeding. Offshore, Wilson's Storm-Petrels and Greater and Sooty Shearwaters arrive by midmonth and can often be found around the feeding whales.

From late June to mid-July, most northern-hemisphere nesters are absent from Cape Cod waters, though a few non-breeding immatures are always a possibility. There can, however, be spectacular concentrations of southern-hemisphere nesters—visiting during what is their nonbreeding season—in particular, Wilson's Storm-Petrels and Greater and Sooty Shearwaters. This is also a good time to see Cory's Shearwaters, in years when they appear this far north, and Manx Shearwaters can be fairly common by the end of July.

Subtle changes begin to occur in the marine environment around mid-August as weak cold fronts begin pushing south. The first of the southbound migrants arrive with these fronts, while the populations of most southern hemisphere nesters begin to decline. Greater Shearwaters remain common, however, and are often the most plentiful species offshore. Gannets, Red-necked Phalaropes, jaegers, and even a few Sabine's Gulls arrive at this time. Parasitic Jaegers can be seen along the coast from Wood End to Race Point in Provincetown, or wherever terns are feeding, while the scarcer Pomarine Jaegers are usually found only well offshore. Manx Shear-waters, Red-necked Phalaropes, and Sabine's Gulls are seen most regularly over the southwest corner of Stellwagen Bank; look for the gulls among the flocks of feeding terns—flocks that can contain thousands of birds, most of which are Common Terns, but with a few Roseate Terns as well.

As the weather continues to cool in September, Northern Fulmars and a few Red Phalaropes may appear offshore. October brings a real shift in the weather as northerly winds occur with increasing regularity. Sea ducks arrive from the north in numbers, and the last of the remaining terns and most shearwaters depart to points south. Any storm-petrels seen at this time are usually Leach's; most of the Wilson's leave by mid-September. Increasing numbers of gannets and kittiwakes arrive, the first Iceland and Glaucous Gulls appear, and Bonaparte's Gulls can be seen along the coast and in the harbors. Jaegers continue to pass through, with an increasing percentage of Pomarine Jaegers as the season wanes.

With November come the alcids. Dovekies, if they appear at all, are most likely at this time, as is the infrequently seen Atlantic Puffin. By the end of the month, Razorbills can be fairly common, and a few murres and guillemots may appear. Gannets and kittiwakes become abundant, sometimes concentrating in spectacular aggregations, both in Cape Cod Bay and offshore. A handful of Greater and Manx

Shearwaters, and Red Phalaropes may linger until midmonth, and the last of the jaegers pass through. By midwinter, only kittiwakes and, in some years, Razorbills are likely to be present in large numbers. A few gannets may linger if the winter is mild, and guillemots are regularly found near shore in Provincetown. See the "Cape Cod Specialties" chapter for more details on the distribution and abundance of the individual species.

Although no sea trips are regularly scheduled from Cape Cod ports after late October, there are usually two or three trips run out of

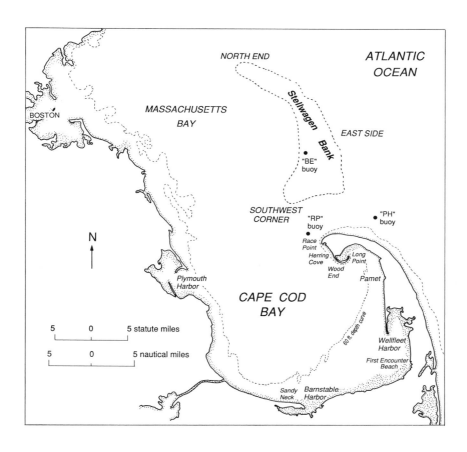

Boston or Plymouth during the late fall and early winter; contact the Massachusetts Audubon Society or the Brookline Bird Club in Boston for possible trips during that time. Both organizations also offer a few all-day sea trips during the warmer months. These longer trips concentrate on finding birds, unlike the shorter, commercial whale watching trips which are geared exclusively to finding and watching whales. Although birds are often found around the whales, this is not always the case. Watching a large concentration of birds on the distant horizon, while the boat sits dead in the water for seemingly endless minutes waiting for a whale to resurface, can be an extremely frustrating experience for a birder. However, only the most jaundiced of birders will fail to find the whales as enjoyable as the birds, if not more so!

The weather at sea is often strikingly different from that on land. Temperatures, particularly in the spring and early summer, can be as much as 15 to 20 degrees colder on the water, and the wind is often appreciably stronger. Dress very warmly, regardless of the season or the weather on land, and wear a waterproof outer layer. If you are prone to seasickness, take medication before leaving land. All of the commercial whale watching boats have sizable, heated cabins, equipped with snack bars.

Those who turn green at the mere thought of stepping onto a boat need not despair of seeing pelagics. Cape Cod, extending 30 miles into the Atlantic as it does, probably offers the best chance anywhere in eastern North America of observing seabirds from land. Because of its location, Provincetown is the most consistently productive area. In almost any season or under any weather conditions, there is a possibility of seeing a few pelagics around the Race Point area, though there are many times when nothing can be found. Northeasterly storms often blow large numbers of pelagics into Cape Cod Bay and several sites, most notably Sandy Neck in Barnstable, Corporation Beach in Dennis, and First Encounter Beach in Eastham, are vantages for seeing these birds during or immediately following a storm. Refer to the appropriate sections in the preceding chapters for more information about these sites.

Be aware that land-based seabirders must often endure extremely adverse weather conditions and be satisfied with distant and often unsatisfactory views of their quarry. However, the spectacle of hundreds or thousands of shearwaters, storm-petrels, gannets, sea ducks, kittiwakes, and others streaming past over a churning sea, if you are fortunate enough to be present to witness it, is reward enough, regardless of how many individual birds go unidentified.

6 CAPE COD SPECIALTIES

This annotated list briefly describes when and where to see a variety of species that visiting birders are typically most interested in finding on Cape Cod. Some are essentially southern species that are near the northern edge of their range here on the Cape, while others are northern species near the southern edge of their range. Also included are a number of seabirds which, although generally erratic and unpredictable in their occurrence, are often more readily found in the waters around Cape Cod than anywhere else on the east coast. The list is by no means all-inclusive, but rather covers the most sought-after birds.

Red-throated Loon A common fall migrant, uncommon winter resident and spring migrant; easy to find in November and early December along most of the Cape Cod Bay shore. Wellfleet Harbor will often provide good, close looks at the species during this season. They are also seen regularly on the ocean side beaches such as Nauset Beach; much less regularly in Nantucket Sound and Buzzards Bay.

Red-necked Grebe A scarce, local, and inconspicuous migrant and winter resident. By far the best location on the Cape to see Red-neckeds and one of the best in the northeast is Corporation Beach in Dennis. A few birds are usually present here from late fall through late winter with numbers increasing, sometimes dramatically, during the early spring, when counts occasionally exceed one hundred. Elsewhere, single birds are infrequently seen along the Cape Cod Bay and ocean shores, with Nauset Beach being one of the better locales to find the species.

Northern Fulmar A common winter resident well offshore but only rarely seen from land, almost exclusively during strong northeasterly blows. Fulmars are occasionally seen on day-long boat trips in the fall and spring, but often the species occurs only beyond the range of these trips.

Cory's Shearwater   An irregular summer and fall visitor. Although often the commonest shearwater in the warm waters south of the Cape, the number of Cory's in Cape waters varies greatly, from nearly absent in some years to fairly common in others. When present, they are seen from land with some regularity.

Greater Shearwater   "The" shearwater in Cape waters, the Greater is generally common to abundant from June into November, and can be expected on most boat trips and from land during storms at locations such as Sandy Neck, First Encounter Beach, and Provincetown.

Sooty Shearwater   A fairly common summer and uncommon fall visitor, the Sooty is the first shearwater to arrive in late May and early June, at which time it often occurs close to shore particularly in Chatham and Provincetown. The species becomes scarce by late summer but a few can usually be found among concentrations of shearwaters through October.

Manx Shearwater   An uncommon summer and fall visitor, most often seen on Stellwagen Bank, where in some years counts may exceed one hundred birds or, during storms, from Sandy Neck or Provincetown.

Leach's Storm-Petrel   The Leach's is a rather rarely seen bird in this area despite the proximity of large nesting colonies along the coast of Maine. The species is highly pelagic, found primarily along the continental shelf far offshore, and during the nesting season becomes very nocturnal. In the Cape area Leach's are most often seen from bayside beaches such as Sandy Neck during strong northeasterly winds from August to early November. They are rarely found on one-day boat trips.

Wilson's Storm-Petrel   The "default" storm-petrel in Cape waters, the Wilson's is common to abundant from late May through August and is seen on virtually all boat trips at this season. The species also can be seen with some regularity from land at locations such as Provincetown, Chatham, and Sandy Neck, particularly during or immediately after periods of fog or onshore winds.

Northern Gannet   One of the true avian spectacles on Cape Cod is the migration of gannets down our coast. The first southbound birds appear in late August and by late October, they are widespread and conspicuous along Cape Cod Bay and ocean beaches. Storms during this season can generate thrilling flights numbering into the many thousands of birds. Gannets generally become scarce by mid-January then increase again in March with the peak of the northbound migration in April. This is an easy species to find during the peak seasons, except along Nantucket Sound where it is normally scarce.

Great Cormorant   A fairly common and increasing winter resident, the largest numbers of Great Cormorants occur along the rocky Cape Cod Canal and Buzzards Bay shores, the oceanside beaches of Chatham, around the Nauset Inlet and marsh, and in Provincetown. Formerly, identifying cormorants in this area involved little more than a glance at the calendar: Double-crested was the warm weather species and Great the cold weather species. However, both species have increased and extended their seasons of occurrence to the point that either is possible at almost any time of the year, although the vast majority from late November through March are Greats and the remainder of the year are Double-cresteds.

Mute Swan   A common resident, easily found on the ponds and bays from Falmouth to Barnstable. The species is still rather scarce, but is increasing, on the Outer Cape.

Brant   A common migrant and winter resident. The largest concentrations of Brant are found in the late fall feeding on the flats along the Cape Cod Bay shore from Brewster to Eastham. They can also be found in Wellfleet Harbor, Nauset Marsh, Pleasant Bay, Barnstable Harbor and various beaches along Nantucket Sound.

Eurasian Wigeon   A very rare but regular migrant and winter visitor. One or two birds are found annually on the ponds of South Monomoy, but otherwise the species is difficult to find. Most recent records away from Monomoy are from the ponds and shallow estuaries of Orleans and Chatham.

Barrow's Goldeneye   A rare but regular winter resident, generally found among the larger concentrations of Common Goldeneyes. The most reliable site has been Pleasant Bay in Chatham, with other traditional sites including Town Cove in Orleans, Stage

Harbor in Chatham and near the mouth of the Bass River in Dennis/Yarmouth.

Harlequin Duck   A rare but fairly regular winter resident, much less common here than along the rocky coasts to the north and south of the area. The only spots where they have been found with any regularity are north of the Nauset Beach parking lot in Orleans and in Wellfleet and Provincetown Harbors. Rarely are more than two or three birds found, and in some years they are absent altogether.

Common Eider   A common to abundant and widespread winter resident, easily found from October through May. Cape Cod lies at the heart of the wintering range for this species, with the shoals off South Monomoy often harboring tens of thousands of individuals. In most years large flocks also can be found in Sandwich near the Cape Cod Canal, at Corporation Beach in Dennis, in Provincetown, around Nauset Inlet and Nauset Beach, in Chatham, and along the rocky shores of Woods Hole.

King Eider   A rare but fairly regular winter visitor, found not only among masses of Common Eiders, but often among flocks of scoters as well. They are not easy to find on Cape Cod, but check near the Cape Cod Canal in Sandwich, at Corporation Beach in Dennis, in Provincetown, and around the rocks at the Nauset Beach parking lot. King Eiders are much more regular visitors north of Boston.

Black Scoter, Surf Scoter and **White-winged Scoter**   All three species of scoters are common to abundant fall migrants with thousands, mostly Surfs and Blacks, passing along Cape Cod Bay shores from mid-September to mid-November. White-wingeds, on the other hand, are much more common along oceanside beaches. During the winter, White-wingeds are generally the most common and widespread, but small numbers of the other two species can usually be found. During this season, look for them at the mouth of the Cape Cod Canal in Sandwich, at Corporation Beach in Dennis, at Herring Cove in Provincetown, at Nauset Beach in Orleans, along the Nantucket Sound shoreline in Chatham and Hyannis, and along the Buzzards Bay coast.

Rough-legged Hawk   A winter visitor in irregular numbers, the Rough-legged Hawk is present almost every year, but is usually quite scarce and hard to find. Rough-leggeds are most often found on the outer Cape, particularly in the Provincetown-Truro area and south of Nauset Beach in Orleans. Also check the Marstons Mills airport. This hawk is much more common on the islands of Nantucket and Martha's Vineyard and in the Newburyport area north of Boston.

Bald Eagle   A rare but regular visitor at any season, seen most frequently on the outer Cape during the late spring and summer. Reports invariably involve immature birds, which wander widely and often frequent the local dumps.

Peregrine Falcon   A regular migrant, particularly in the fall, and a rare but recently regular winter resident. This magnificent bird is encountered almost exclusively along the immediate coast, particularly in areas where shorebirds and waterfowl congregrate. Monomoy is especially favored, but Nauset Beach in Orleans, Coast Guard Beach in Eastham, Sandy Neck in Barnstable, and Provincetown are all locations of regular sightings.

Northern Bobwhite   A common year-round resident. The cheerful whistle of the Bobwhite is still a frequently heard sound in the less-developed, open areas of the Cape. Bobwhites are easy to locate when they are calling in the spring and early summer but can be difficult to find during the remainder of the year. The Crane Wildlife Management Area in Falmouth, the Marstons Mills airport, and the Wellfleet Bay Wildlife Sanctuary are some areas particularly favored by these quail. During the winter Bobwhites form small coveys of 6 to 20 birds and often frequent bird feeders.

American Oystercatcher   A common summer resident on Monomoy, oystercatchers are rare and local elsewhere, although slowly increasing. Other than on Monomoy and Morris Island in Chatham, the only area where oystercatchers are seen regulary is in the southern portion of Nauset Marsh. When present, they are generally noisy and conspicuous.

Piping Plover   This Federally Threatened species, though much reduced in numbers, is still a fairly common nesting species in this area, with roughly half of the state's 130-plus pairs occupying sites on Cape Cod. The largest populations are found at Sandy Neck in Barnstable and on Coast Guard Beach in Eastham, but most of the barrier beaches support a pair or two. Use the utmost discretion when approaching nesting sites of this species and, when encountering birds that appear agitated, give them a wide berth!

Migrant Shorebirds   Though any estuary or tidal flat will produce a few shorebirds during migration periods from early April through early June and early July through early November, Monomoy island is the shorebird capital of Cape Cod. The Nauset marsh system supports comparable numbers but is more difficult to cover and has fewer of the larger, less common species. Other spots that are worth checking include the Sandy Neck/Barnstable Harbor area, the Wellfleet Bay Wildlife Sanctuary, Morris Island in Chatham, West Dennis Beach, and South Cape Beach in Mashpee.

Curlew Sandpiper   A very rare and irregular migrant, most often seen on Monomoy and, less frequently, in the Nauset area. This species is found only once every two or three years on average; they are a more regular visitor in the Newburyport area north of Boston.

Buff-breasted Sandpiper   A rare but regular fall migrant, found from late August to late September. The Buff-breasted is most often seen on Monomoy, but Coast Guard Beach in Eastham is another good spot. Very rarely seen on mud flats with other shorebirds, Buff-breasteds prefer dry, open areas in the upper parts of salt marshes or Hudsonia moors in dune hollows. Look particularly along the wrack line at the dune/marsh interface.

Hudsonian Godwit   A regular fall migrant on Monomoy where it is easily found from early July into early September. Elsewhere the species appears sporadically and is difficult to find. If you are unable to get to Monomoy, check around Morris Island in Chatham at low tide or the Nauset Marsh area where a few godwits are occasionally seen.

Ruff   A very rare migrant. One or two are found somewhere on the Cape just about every year. Most records are from Monomoy, the Nauset area, and the Wellfleet Bay Wildlife Sanctuary. Ruffs are found more frequently in the Newburyport area north of Boston during the spring.

Red-necked Phalarope   A regular migrant offshore, seen in small numbers on Stellwagen Bank off Provincetown in late May and again from late July into September. Occasionally one or two individuals will show up on mud flats among other migrant shorebirds, particularly during the late summer. Phalaropes, often in flocks, can also be seen from land at times during easterly blows.

Red Phalarope   A regular migrant far offshore, The Red Phalarope is more pelagic than the Red-necked and much less frequently seen on Stellwagen Bank or from land. Your best chance of seeing one from land is during an easterly blow; otherwise they occur primarily along the continental slope beyond the range of one-day boat trips.

Parasitic Jaeger, Pomarine Jaeger and **Long-tailed Jaeger**   Cape Cod offers the birder one of the best chances anywhere on the East Coast of seeing jaegers from land, although numbers vary from year to year depending upon the food supply. The Parasitic is by far the most likely species to be seen from land. Pomarine Jaegers are more common offshore but can occasionally be seen from land, particularly after easterly blows. The Long-tailed Jaeger is extremely rare onshore and seldom seen even at sea. Provincetown is generally the most productive location for finding jaegers, especially when there are flocks of feeding terns present. The Monomoy/Chatham area also offers fairly good prospects for seeing these spectacular aerial pirates. During fall storms, flocks of jaegers often get blown into Cape Cod Bay and can be seen from such locations as Sandy Neck in Barnstable, Corporation Beach in Dennis, and First Encounter Beach in Eastham. Jaegers are notoriously difficult to identify, and also beware of immature Laughing Gulls in late summer, which often look and behave similarly.

Little Gull   A rare but regular spring and fall migrant, the Little Gull is almost always found among flocks of Bonaparte's Gulls. Monomoy in the late spring is one of the best bets to find this tiny larid. From the late fall to early winter, look anywhere along the Cape Cod Bay shore, in Provincetown, around Morris Island in Chatham, and the Woods Hole shoreline. However, Little Gulls seldom linger in any one spot on the Cape and require some luck to find.

Common Black-headed Gull   A rare migrant and winter visitor, generally found in protected estuaries, often in association with flocks of Bonaparte's Gulls or Ring-billed Gulls. A pair nested on Monomoy in 1984, the first U.S. nesting to be recorded, and one or two birds continue to be seen there in the spring. Otherwise, they have been seen in a number of areas from one end of the Cape to the other. Usually one or two birds are present every winter, and wintering individuals often return to the same area for two or three consecutive years.

Iceland Gull A regular winter visitor in small numbers from December through March. The Provincetown area, particularly Provincetown Harbor, is by far the most reliable locale and counts of four to five individuals are not unusual there. Other spots where the species is seen with some regularity are the mouth of the Cape Cod Canal in Sandwich, the Chatham Fish Pier, and in Woods Hole. Any concentration of wintering gulls, including those at the local dumps, can have an Iceland or two.

Lesser Black-backed Gull   A rare fall migrant and very rare winter visitor and spring migrant. Most sightings are from the outer Cape among the large concentrations of gulls at places such as Race Point in Provincetown, the Nauset area in Eastham, and Monomoy. Look for this species among flocks of Herring Gulls, often at the periphery, and usually *not* among Great Black-backed Gulls.

Glaucous Gull   A rare but regular winter visitor, found in the same areas as Iceland Gulls, the Glaucous Gull is much the rarer of the two species. Most reports are of immature birds.

Black-legged Kittiwake An abundant winter resident offshore and regularly seen from land, often in large numbers when food is abundant or after easterly blows. A few individuals are often found hanging around fishing ports such as Provincetown Harbor, the Chatham Fish Pier, and the mouth of the Cape Cod Canal. Kittiwakes are usually quite rare in Nantucket Sound and Buzzards Bay. In some years, a few immatures linger into the early summer, concentrating at Provincetown, Coast Guard Beach, and Monomoy.

Sabine's Gull   A rare but regular fall migrant and a very rare spring migrant offshore. Most reports have come from Stellwagen Bank where the species is typically seen in August or September, associating with flocks of feeding terns. On very rare occasions an individual will show up on land among flocks of terns or small gulls. Otherwise, land-based observations are primarily of birds seen along the Cape Cod Bay shore during or immediately after easterly gales.

Roseate Tern An uncommon and very local breeder and a common to abundant post-breeding visitor. Small numbers of this Federally Endangered species usually nest at Gray's Beach in Yarmouth, on New Island in Orleans, and on Monomoy. Large concentrations, indeed a substantial percentage of the Roseate Terns in the Northeast, begin to appear on the Cape in late July and remain into mid-September. Peak numbers are generally found on Monomoy, in the Nauset area and in Provincetown, but fluctuate annually depending on local food supplies.

Arctic Tern   A rather rare, local, and decreasing nester, and an uncommon spring migrant and summer visitor. Only a few pairs of Arctic Terns remain on the Cape, most in the New Island/Nauset Beach area of Orleans. Also a pair or two usually attempt to nest on Monomoy each year. A small number of adult Arctics pass through the outer Cape, particularly Monomoy and the Nauset area, during May and early June. In recent years, numbers of nonbreeding one- and two year-old birds have been present from late June into early August, with the largest concentrations occurring on Monomoy, in the Nauset area, and in Provincetown. All Arctic Terns leave promptly in mid-August and the species is very rarely seen after the end of August.

Least Tern   A common and widespread nester, with colonies of varying size occurring in many areas along the Cape's coastlines. Least Tern colonies tend to be rather ephemeral, but some of the more reliable traditional sites include Kalmus Park in Hyannis, West Dennis Beach in Dennis, Harding's Beach and South Beach Island in Chatham, Nauset Beach in Orleans, Coast Guard Beach in Eastham, the Race Point area of Provincetown, Sandy Neck in Barnstable, and the Old Harbor/Scortons Creek area of Sandwich. This remarkable little bird is the only of the Cape's four nesting tern species to have historically maintained a stable population in the area.

Dovekie   A very irregular late fall migrant and winter visitor, which seems to have become much less regular than in years past. Dovekies are most likely to be seen along Cape Cod Bay beaches during or immediately after easterly blows in November and December. Occasionally a bird or two will show up in sheltered bays or harbors such as in Provincetown Harbor or Wellfleet Harbor.

Common Murre   A rare winter visitor, most likely to be found off of Race Point in Provincetown or in Provincetown Harbor. Curiously, despite the rarity of sightings of this species from land, it is one of the alcids most commonly found oiled on Cape Cod beaches.

Thick-billed Murre   Usually a rare winter visitor, but in some years the species can be found with some frequency. As with all the alcids, the most likely spot to see them is Provincetown, either at Race Point or in the harbor, but sightings are also possible anywhere along the Cape Cod Bay shore during easterly storms or along oceanside beaches at almost any time.

Razorbill   An uncommon winter resident, but usually by far the most common of the alcids in Cape Cod waters. At least a few are found every year, and when food supplies are plentiful, counts into the hundreds or even thousands are not unusual. Provincetown is the best place to see Razorbills, but they are often found along oceanside beaches as well, and good flights can occur along the Cape Cod Bay shore during easterly gales. Peak numbers generally are present from late November into early January.

Black Guillemot   Usually a rare and local winter visitor, but the species seems to have increased during the past decade. By far the most reliable place to see guillemots is the Race Point area of Provincetown where counts of over one hundred birds have occasionally been made in some recent winters; elsewhere the species is very scarce but sometimes found along Cape Cod Bay and ocean beaches.

Atlantic Puffin   A very rare and irregular winter visitor. Puffins, when seen, are usually found in the same places as the other alcids (see above), but they are by far the rarest of the six species. In some years, a few Puffins are reported from Stellwagen Bank in the late fall.

Snowy Owl   A rare and irregular winter visitor, and a bird that is not seen every year. The most likely areas to find Snowy Owls include the Provincetown dunes, Nauset Beach in Orleans, Monomoy, and Sandy Neck in Barnstable, but any barrier beach may host one. This dramatic bird is always much more common from Boston northward.

Short-eared Owl   A rather rare, local, and decreasing nester, and a rare to uncommon migrant and winter visitor. Nesting is currently known to occur only on Monomoy, but has been suspected on Nauset Beach in Orleans as well. Winterers and migrants may appear on any barrier beach or large open area.

Northern Saw-whet Owl   A rare and local nester, and a regular migrant and winter resident in varying numbers. This appealing little owl nests in a few places on the Cape, usually in close associ- ation with Atlantic white cedar swamps. The cedar swamp at the Marconi site in South Wellfleet is a favored spot as is Nickerson State Park in Brewster, especially south of Cliff Pond. Migrants and winterers may occur in almost any dense stand of evergreens.

Whip-poor-will   A common but increasingly local breeding spe- cies. Once one of the most common summer night sounds on the Cape, the loud, persistent call of the Whip-poor-will has vanished from many areas. The species is still common anywhere that extensive, undisturbed woodlands exist, such as the pine barrens within the Cape Cod National Seashore in Wellfleet and Truro, Nickerson State Park in Brewster, the Barnstable Conservation Area in Marstons Mills, or the Crane Wildlife Management Area in Falmouth.

Carolina Wren   An uncommon year-round resident, which inhab- its dense, overgrown thickets and tangles. Carolina Wrens are most common in the Falmouth area; try the thickets behind town hall. They regularly occur east to Eastham, but are usually rather rare from Wellfleet northward.

Northern Shrike   An irregular winter visitor, which varies from vir- tually absent in some years to fairly common in major flight years. They can be found in a variety of open habitats and are most common on the outer Cape. Some of the more reliable spots are Provincetown, particularly around the airport and the seashore vis- itor's center, the Pilgrim Heights/High Head area in North Truro, the Bound Brook area in Wellfleet, Fort Hill in Eastham, the Pochet area in East Orleans, and Sandy Neck in Barnstable.

Migrant Land Birds   One of the features of birding on Cape Cod is the occurrence of waves of migrant flycatchers, vireos, warblers, sparrows, and others during the spring and fall. When conditions are right, thousands upon thousands of songbirds appear in favored areas. Sadly, however, waves of any magnitude seem to have become less and less frequent as habitat destruction and other factors, most of which remain speculative, diminish our avifauna.

In the spring, what constitutes "prime conditions" on the Cape remains difficult to define with any certainty, but generally warm southwesterly winds, particularly those associated with the northward passage of a warm front up the Atlantic seaboard, generate the best flights. However, significant waves of migrants have been recorded during a wide variety of weather conditions, including raw, damp northeasterly winds. Hence, the best rule of thumb is simply to get out and look every morning, otherwise you may miss the "big one!" The premier spot for observing spring migration on the Cape is the Beech Forest in Provincetown. Other good locations include the Pilgrim Heights/High Head area in North Truro, the Wellfleet Bay Wildlife Sanctuary, Pochet Island in East Orleans, Dennis Pond in Yarmouth, the fish hatchery in Sandwich and Beebe Woods in Falmouth.

In the fall, the best birding generally follows winds out of the northwest with cool temperatures, typical of conditions associated with the passage of a cold front. When a front stalls just offshore, some of the greatest concentrations of migrants often occur. During this season, Provincetown is again one of the better areas for migrants, including not only the Beech Forest but the many thickets in the area, such as those around the airport. Other places worth checking are the High Head area in North Truro, the Wellfleet Bay Wildlife Sanctuary, the Marconi Site in South Wellfleet, primarily for sparrows, Pochet Island in East Orleans, Morris Island in Chatham (most of which is privately owned and generally off-limits to visiting birders, unfortunately), and Monomoy.

Northern Parula A rather rare and local breeder, a common spring migrant, and an uncommon fall migrant. The only nesting parulas in the state are found on Cape Cod and the adjacent Elizabeth Islands. The population has declined considerably and the species is now listed under the category of "Special Concern" on the state's endangered and threatened species list. Remnant populations persist along the Mashpee River in Mashpee, Bumps River in Osterville, and in the West Harwich conservation area. They are usually found at the fringes of Atlantic white cedar swamps. Migrants are found in the typical land bird traps listed above.

Pine Warbler A very common and widespread nester in the pine barrens and mixed pine/oak woodlands, a common spring migrant, and an uncommon fall migrant. The musical trill of the Pine Warbler is one of the most frequent sounds in most of the Cape's woodlands, and the visiting birder should have no trouble locating this species during the spring and early summer. Pine Warblers become much more difficult to find once they stop singing in midsummer but usually can be located by diligent searching in the pine barrens for roving, mixed-species flocks of passerines. A few Pine Warblers attempt to winter in most years, when they most often show up at suet feeders.

Prairie Warbler A common nester in overgrown fields and scrubby pine barrens, and a fairly common migrant. The Prairie Warbler is widespread and easy to find during the summer in areas with extensive growth of red cedar or dry, sparse stands of pitch pine. Some good sites are the Crane Wildlife Management Area in Falmouth, the Marstons Mills airport, Fort Hill in Eastham, the Wellfleet Bay Wildlife Sanctuary, the Marconi Site in South Wellfleet, and around the Cape Cod National Seashore visitor center in Provincetown.

Grasshopper Sparrow A rare and local nester, which has declined drastically over the past half century and which is now in danger of disappearing altogether as a breeder on the Cape. The only nesting sites remaining are the Crane Wildlife Management Area in Falmouth, which supports several pairs, and the Otis Air Force Base, which is off-limits to visiting birders.

Seaside Sparrow An uncommon and very local nester and a rather rare fall migrant and winter visitor. The only consistent area for nesting Seasides is the Great Marsh in Barnstable, where at least several pairs are usually present. In some years, they have been found during the breeding season on Monomoy, in the Nauset marsh, and at the Wellfleet Bay Wildlife Sanctuary, but they are more often absent from these areas. The best chance for finding the species during the fall and early winter is Fort Hill in Eastham during times when abnormally high tides flood the marsh and force both Seaside and Sharp-tailed Sparrows out of the marsh and into the grass and shrubs at the base of the hill. Under these conditions you might also have some luck around the edge of the marsh at First Encounter Beach in Eastham or at the end of Navigation Road in Barnstable. You will probably have to get your feet wet to see this bird!

Vesper Sparrow A rare and local nester and fall migrant, the Vesper Sparrow, like the Grasshopper Sparrow, was once widespread on the Cape but has now all but vanished as a breeder. The only known nesting sites remaining are the Marconi Site in South Wellfleet and some of the more vegetated dunes around Provincetown and in the Pilgrim Heights area in North Truro. Vespers can usually be found in these areas into mid-October.

Lapland Longspur An uncommon fall migrant and winter visitor, most often found among flocks of Horned Larks or Snow Buntings that frequent the short grass areas along barrier beaches. Some of the best spots are the Race Point/Provincetown airport area, Nauset Beach in Orleans, the beach at the end of Morris Island in Chatham, Monomoy, Chapin Beach in Yarmouth, and Sandy Neck in Barnstable.

Snow Bunting A common late fall migrant and uncommon winter resident, which typically frequents areas of extensive dunes along the outer beaches. Good locations to find them include the dunes along the oceanside from Provincetown to North Truro, Coast Guard Beach in Eastham, Nauset Beach in Orleans, Monomoy, Harding's Beach in Chatham, Chapin Beach in Yarmouth, and Sandy Neck.

INDEX